What's Missing Inside You?

Discover the leading character in the story of your life

Paul Schlieker

What's Missing Inside You?
Discover the leading character in the story of your life
by Paul Schlieker

Printed in the United States of America

ISBN 9781600345180

www.xulonpress.com

Contents

§

Acknowledgement

§

In recent years, authors have become my mentors. The spiritual writings of A.B. Simpson and A.W. Tozer have significantly shaped my view of God, the world and myself. Although no longer living, their influence still lives. God has used them to transform the message and mission of my life.

Many gifted people offered me valuable insights that contributed to writing this workbook. I want to express a special word of thanks to Merlyn Klaus for his vision, Dale Burklund for his passion and above all, Peggy (my wife). Her discernment and emotional support are a gift from God.

Open Your Heart Series

§

Each computer is built with an operating system that runs the various software applications such as Word, Excel and QuickBooks.

Discipleship is the operating system of the church. Jesus built his operating system by creating a discipling culture. Discipleship is life-on-life transformation. From Jesus, we learn that success is not about size. Success is succession.

The *Open your Heart Series* offers four distinct studies that are uniquely designed to introduce Christianity, explain foundational principles, create authentic disciples and train disciple-makers. These ready-to-use materials include discussion questions and a leader guide. They are perfect for individuals, small groups and classes of any size.

Study 1 – Bible Basics

Bible Basics is for those who don't know what the Bible is…let alone what it's all about. This study assumes no Bible knowledge or background. These six full color lessons identify fundamental truths about God, the Bible, Satan, Sin and Jesus.

Study 2 – What's Missing Inside You?

Do you want to discover foundational principles for Christian living? *What's Missing Inside You?* will benefit people at all stages of faith. This study answers two questions: What does Jesus have to do with me? and Does God have a plan for my life? Starting at square one, thirteen lessons explore important topics such as God's existence, man's purpose, forgiveness, temptation, the Holy Spirit, and much more. You will love the clear Scriptural teaching, practical application and over fifty real life stories.

Study 3 – Kingdom Disciple

Is there a difference between a *Christian* and a *follower of Jesus?* What is a disciple? What does Jesus really expect? These are a few of the questions that are answered in *Kingdom Disciple – Building Your Relationship with Jesus*. This five-lesson study is not a new program about "doing discipleship." It is a guide to create authentic disciples. It is for those who are ready to do whatever it takes to become like Christ.

Study 4 – Kingdom-Driven Discipleship

Why is it important to make disciples where you live, work and play? Have you ever considered your job as a kingdom assignment, or your office as a kingdom outpost? *Kingdom-Driven Discipleship – Making Disciples in the Middle of the Harvest Field* equips disciples to be disciple-makers. This five-lesson study is excellent training for seasoned believers.

Visit our Website – www.bible-study-lesson-plans.com

All four books are available at www.bible-study-lesson-plans.com. To learn more, read online what others say about these discipleship books. In addition, many free resources are available including our discipleship newsletter, small group leader training, devotions, Sunday school lessons, audio sermons and more.

If you can read it, you can lead it!

Intent of This Study

§

This study is about you and God. It invites you to form a *relationship* with God and challenges you to *represent* God in the world. This material aims to help ordinary people recognize that life is more than family, friends, work and retirement. It is for those who can't put their finger on it, but deep down have a gnawing suspicion that something's missing.

The intent of this study is to answer two questions: *What does Jesus have to do with me?* and *Does God have a plan for my life?* The missing pieces of your life will fall into place as you take a fresh look at foundational principles for Christian living.

Based on the teachings of the Bible, you will recognize that none of us is the leading character in the story of our life. You will discover that what is missing inside you is *God Himself.*

In his book, *The Pursuit of God,* A. W. Tozer writes, "When religion has said its last word, there is little we need other than God Himself." This study will give you a basis to trust God, reasons to love God and the motivation to obey God.

Lessons 1-6 will develop your personal relationship with God. Lessons 7-13 explore the reason God made you and how to be His representative. You will discover eight life-changing insights that will transform the way you see God, yourself and your future:

God is . . .	Your Father	You are . . .	His Child
	Your Savior		His Temple
	Your Guide		His Disciple
	Your King		His Representative

Getting the Most from This Study

§

Layout

What's Missing Inside You? is composed of thirteen lessons. It explains foundational principles for Christian living. The teaching is clear and easy to understand.

Structure

This book is designed for a group setting. You will benefit from the wisdom and insights of other people. A small group is best suited to create a climate of trust. If you have a mid-size group, consider having members sit at tables or form smaller circles.

Preparation

Read the assigned lesson, complete the *Individual Response Questions,* and do the *Personal Assessment* prior to your group meeting. The questions and the assessment are the basis of your group discussion. Advance preparation will help you personally engage.

Timetable

Jesus taught people, not lessons. If necessary, devote multiple sessions to one lesson.

Resources

Use these additional resources found at the end of the study:

- Leader Guide
- Lesson Summary
- Bible People Index

Spiritual Terms

§

Bible

The word *Bible* means a collection of writings. It is derived from Latin and Greek words that mean "books." The Bible (also called the Scripture and God's Word) is a library of sixty-six books. It is divided into two parts: the *Old Testament* and the *New Testament*.

The word *testament* means covenant. Covenant is a relationship word. Human beings are created to be *one with God* – to know and walk with God now and forever. Similar to a marriage relationship, a covenant is a mutual and total commitment between two people.

Because of sin, the original relationship between God and man was broken. God's plan to rebuild and restore this relationship was first revealed to Abraham. Years later, Moses gave the nation of Israel a fuller understanding of what it means to love and obey the Lord. The essence of Israel's covenant relationship with God is best summarized by the Ten Commandments.

As God's Son, Jesus came to earth to establish an everlasting covenant between God and man – once and for all. Jesus called it the *new covenant*. This new covenant is the full expression of God's love for all people. Jesus taught that people do not become "one with God" by merely keeping commandments, but by receiving God's grace.

The death of Jesus on the cross and the blood he shed for the sins of the world is the heart of the new covenant. Jesus Himself is the free gift of God's grace. We enter into an eternal covenant relationship with God by placing our trust in Jesus. Knowing, loving and walking with Jesus is the same as knowing, loving and walking with God. In short, this is the Bible's central message.

The thirty-nine books of the Old Testament were originally written in Hebrew and cover the creation of the world until around 400 BC. The twenty-seven books of the New Testament were originally written in Greek and cover Jesus' birth until around AD 95.

The Bible originated with God. He spoke it into existence. God would be a stranger to us if He had not spoken. II Timothy 3:16 says, *All Scripture is God-breathed.* This means that the Bible came from God's mouth. When you read the Bible you can hear God's voice. The Bible is more than a book that was once written – it is a *voice* that is speaking here and now.

The Bible is God's autobiography. It is God's revelation about Himself. To understand it, we must read the Scriptures as God's revelation, not as a religious Wikipedia.

The Bible explains who God is, what God values and how God works. It reveals that God is the Creator, Father, Savior, King, and Judge of all the earth. Behind every word that anybody utters is the person who speaks it. God's Word has authority because of who He is.

The Bible is personal. It contains principles to guide, commands to obey, warnings to heed, examples to emulate and promises to claim. The Scriptures are designed to enter our hearts and form us into people who reflect the likeness of Jesus. The greatest portion of God's Word is devoted to persuading people to alter their ways and align their lives with God. For the Bible to be helpful we must approach it with an open mind, a tender heart and a surrendered will.

The Bible is about human beings relating to God and to one another. It is relevant; it is not "dated." It is a living message for the contemporary world.

The Bible is universal. It is not limited to any particular generation, culture or nation. It is a message for all people. *Everything that is written in the past was written to teach us, so that through endurance and the encouragement of the Scriptures we might have hope* (Romans 15:4).

In A. B. Simpson's timeless personal testimony, *Himself,* he describes seeing a copy of the Constitution of the United States skillfully engraved in a copper plate. When he looked at it closely, it was simply a piece of writing. But when he stood back and looked at it from a distance, it was the face of George Washington. Simpson said, "At a distance, the face shown out in the shading of the letters and I saw a person, not the words or the ideas." He believed this is the way to view the Bible – not to see mere ideas, but rather, to see Jesus Himself.

Father, Son, Holy Spirit

God is both one *and* three. God exists eternally in three unchanging beings or persons. The three names for God are: God the Father, Jesus the Son (also called Christ), and the Holy Spirit. The Bible refers to all three as God. They all have the characteristics, qualities and power of God because they are God. The names *God, Jesus* and *Holy Spirit* are often used together.

II Corinthians 3:14	May the grace of the Lord Jesus Christ, the love of God, and the fellowship of the Holy Spirit, be with you all.

Biblical Christianity is not principle-centered, it is *person-centered*. Christianity is a Living Person, *living in,* a living person; Somebody *living in* somebody – God indwelling man. The Scriptures refer to God, Jesus and the Holy Spirit living *in* us.

I John 4:16	God is love. Whoever lives in love lives in God, and God in him.
Ephesians 3:16-17	I pray that he may strengthen you with power through his Spirit in your inner being, so that Christ may dwell in your hearts through faith.
I Corinthians 6:19	Do you not know that your body is a temple of the Holy Spirit, who is in you, whom you received from God?
II Corinthians 13:5	Examine yourselves to see whether you are in the faith; test yourselves. Do you not realize that Christ Jesus lives in you?

Satan, the devil

Satan is the great adversary of God and man. In the Bible, Satan is often called the devil (which means *the slanderer*). The origin of Satan is uncertain, but the Bible implies that he was once an angel who fell under condemnation because of ambitious pride (Isaiah 14:12-15). In his fall, Satan drew spiritual agents with him. These are called his angels, demons and evil spirits.

Satan is engaged in a worldwide, unrelenting struggle against God and all goodness. He is ever-seeking to defeat God's plans and seduce people to evil and ruin. Though Satan is not all-powerful like God, the biblical portrait of Satan is a spiritual being, highly intelligent, immensely powerful and utterly corrupt. Jesus believed in his existence and warned of his power.

Satan is real. Satan is most deceptive when he persuades people that he does not exist. Satan is a defeated enemy. God is the ultimate authority in the universe, not the devil. Jesus promised that eternal fire is prepared for the devil. *And the devil who deceived them was thrown into the lake of burning sulfur…and will be tormented day and night forever and ever* (Revelation 20:10).

Follower of Jesus

In this study, the term *Christian* is used sparingly for two reasons. First, *Christian* occurs only three times in the Bible and Jesus never used the word. Second, in Western culture the term *Christian* is either misunderstood or void of meaning.

Some Americans regard Christians as simply a political base of voters. Furthermore, while some view Christians as generous and loving, others view them as self-righteous and judgmental.

For clarification, the term used in this study for "Christian" is *follower of Jesus*. **A Christian is a follower of Jesus who is devoted to God's work in the world.**

Lesson 1 – The God Who Is

§

Is There a God?

On April 12, 1961, aboard *Vostok I*, Soviet cosmonaut Yuri Gagarin became the first person in history to orbit the earth. After Gagarin returned he was asked, "Did you see God?" His response was, "No, I didn't see God. I looked and looked but I didn't see God."

Seven years later, aboard *Apollo 8,* American astronauts Frank Borman, James Lovell and William Anders, began a one hundred forty-seven hour mission – the first mission to orbit the moon. They celebrated Christmas Eve in orbit. On December 24, 1968, a different message was delivered:

> We are now approaching lunar sunrise. And for all the people on Earth, the crew of *Apollo 8* has a message that we would like to send to you: In the beginning God created the heaven and the earth...and God saw that it was good. From the crew of *Apollo 8,* we close with good night and Merry Christmas. And God bless all of you on the good Earth.

Is there any proof of God? When it comes to the possibility of God's existence, the Bible says that while everyone has enough evidence, some have suppressed the truth (Romans 1:19-21). But for those who want to know if God is real He says, *You will seek me and find me; when you seek me with all your heart, I will be found by you* (Jeremiah 29:13-14). Before you consider the evidence surrounding the existence of God, honestly ask yourself this question: *If God does exist, would I want to know Him?*

The Seeker's Prayer

The first book of the Bible is called *Genesis*. Genesis means *beginnings*. The first four words of the Bible are, *In the beginning God...* (Genesis 1:1). In his book *Basic Christianity,* British preacher and author John Stott writes,

> You can never take God by surprise. You can never anticipate Him. He always makes the first move. He is always there 'in the beginning.' Before man existed, God acted. Before man stirs himself to seek God, God has sought man. In the Bible we do not see man groping after God; we see God reaching after man. The chief reason why people do not know God is not because He hides from them, but because they hide from Him.

You will find God when you seek Him with all your heart. Come to terms with this reality: **People who passionately seek God find Him.** The good news is that God is on your side. He wants to be found by you. Let God know how determined you are. In *Basic Christianity,* John Stott recommends this prayer to guide your search:

> God, if you exist (and I don't know if you do), and if you can hear this prayer (and I don't know if you can), I want to tell you that I am an honest seeker after the truth. Show me if Jesus is your Son and the Savior of the world. And if you bring conviction to my mind, I will trust him as my Savior and follow him as my Lord. Amen.

Evidences of God's Existence

1. People in all cultures have been convinced there is a God

Anthropological research indicates that there is a universal belief in God. The earliest histories and legends around the world suggest a belief in "one God," even in today's polytheistic societies.

2. The complexity of our planet points to an intelligent Designer

The earth is the right distance from the sun. If the earth were any further away from the sun we would all freeze; any closer and we would burn up. The earth remains this perfect distance while it rotates around the sun at a speed of 67,000 miles per hour. It also rotates on its axis, allowing the entire surface of the earth to be properly warmed and cooled every day.

The moon is the perfect size and distance from the earth for its gravitational pull. The moon creates important ocean tides and movement so ocean waters do not stagnate. At the same time, it restrains our massive oceans from flooding the continents.

The human brain processes more than a million messages per second. Your brain weighs the important data and filters out the relatively unimportant. This screening function is what allows you to focus and operate effectively in the world. It takes a mind more intelligent than man's to create the human brain.

3. Mere "chance" is not an adequate explanation for creation

Material things do not exist by chance. Imagine a massive explosion at a local newspaper company containing computers, paper, ink and printing presses. What are the chances that such an explosion could create a perfectly typed publication? Could our complex world come about by chance?

4. The sense of right and wrong cannot be biologically explained

All people in every culture have a universal feeling of right and wrong. If an innocent child is harmed, there is a desire to confront that act as evil. Where did people get this sense of rightness and wrongness? How do we explain this universal conscience?

5. God has revealed Himself through Jesus and the Bible

God's thoughts and attitudes have been revealed. We don't have to wonder what God is like. His written Word and Jesus, His Son, tell us all we need to know.

Seeking God

Abraham was an ordinary man who wanted to find God. In Genesis 12:1, Abraham was called by God to leave his country and his relatives to be the father of the Jewish nation (around 1950 BC). Through Abraham, God promised to bless all nations on earth. To *bless* means to provide for, prosper and make joyful. The Scriptures teach, *Without faith it is impossible to please God, because anyone who comes to him must believe that he exists and that he rewards those who earnestly seek him* (Hebrews 11:6). One thing we know about Abraham before God called him was that **he had a seeking heart.**

Although Abraham didn't know God, he was still looking. Since he didn't know the true God, he *worshiped other gods* (Joshua 24:2). Abraham was looking for God and the Lord rewarded his search. Abraham's relationship with God grew very close. Three times in the Bible Abraham is called a *friend of God* (II Chronicles 20:7; Isaiah 41:8; James 2:23).

God can recognize a seeking heart. He can see your heart right now. Today, God is still looking for those who want to know Him. *The eyes of the Lord range throughout the earth to strengthen those whose hearts are fully committed to him* (II Chronicles 16:9).

As God revealed Himself, Abraham was quickly confronted with two realities: *The Lord is the only true God,* and *other gods are not real and must not be worshiped.* Throughout Scripture, the Lord reminds us of these two truths:

The Lord is the Only God

Deuteronomy 4:39	Acknowledge and take to heart this day that the Lord is God in heaven above and on earth below. There is no other.
Isaiah 45:5-6	I am the Lord, and there is no other; apart from me there is no God.
Mark 12:32	"Well said, teacher," the man replied. "You are right in saying that God is one and there is no other but him."
I Corinthians 8:4, 6	We know that an idol is nothing at all in the world and that there is no God but one. For us there is but one God, the Father, from whom all things came and for whom we live; and there is but one Lord, Jesus Christ, through whom all things came and through whom we live.

Do Not Worship Other "gods"

Exodus 20:3	You shall have no other gods before me.
Deuteronomy 12:31	You must not worship the Lord your God in their way, because in worshiping their gods, they do all kinds of detestable things the Lord hates.
Psalm 16:4	The sorrows of those will increase who run after other gods.

Matthew 4:10	Jesus said to him, "Away from me Satan! For it is written: 'Worship the Lord your God, and serve him only.'"
I John 5:20-21	Dear children, keep yourselves from idols.

Idolatry

An idol is an image or a statue fashioned to be an object of worship. God prohibits making any image or statue to represent Him. Idols are often made out of wood or stone. **Idols are forbidden because they are misleading, powerless and misplace our worship.** God accepts the diversity of cultures, but not diversity of religions.

Serving and worshiping false gods is prohibited. God is a jealous God and He will not tolerate any rivals. *I am the Lord; that is my name! I will not give my glory to another or my praise to idols* (Isaiah 42:8). Idolatry was rampant in the days of Isaiah the prophet (730 BC). God instructed His people to follow Him and forsake their idols:

> *This is what the Lord says – Israel's King and Redeemer, the Lord Almighty: I am the first and I am the last; apart from me there is no God. All who make idols are nothing and the things they treasure are worthless. The carpenter cuts down a tree and fashions a god and worships it; he makes an idol and bows down to it. Half of the wood he burns in the fire; over it he prepares his meal, he roasts his meat and eats his fill. He warms himself and says, 'Ah, I am warm; I see the fire.'*
>
> *From the rest he makes a god, his idol; he bows down to it and worships. He prays to it and says, 'Save me; you are my god.' No one stops to think, no one has the knowledge or understanding to say, 'Half of it I used for fuel; shall I make a detestable thing from what is left? Shall I bow down to a block of wood?'* (Isaiah 44:6, 9, 13, 16-17, 19)

Idols Today

Idols do not need to be statues. **An idol is anything we believe we need apart from God to make us happy, satisfied or fulfilled.** Idols today are often revealed by what we fear, desire or trust. When people turn away from the true God, they experience a need or deficiency. To fill their emptiness, people turn their attention to the things they believe will meet the need. Whatever fills your need may seem innocent until it starts to rule your life.

Though not made of wood or stone, they become *heart-idols* when we place more importance on them than God. This means we **fear, desire** or **trust** them more than the one true God. Whenever we believe that something other than God has the power to give us what we lack, we begin to experience the loss of clear thinking. The following list is a sample of modern day heart-idols:

I Fear...

- People's rejection, attacks or control
- Losing or not gaining a reputation
- My boss firing me or getting angry at me
- My children turning out badly
- My spouse / friend betraying me
- Losing an inheritance / losing control
- Sickness / death
- Punishment / failure

I Desire...

- To feel good (eat, drink, drugs, sex, TV)
- Freedom from financial constraints
- Admiration / recognition / success
- Nice house / material goods
- That my children be responsible
- That my spouse / friend love me
- That circumstances be different

I Trust...

- Drinking / gambling (to escape frustrations and boredom)
- Sex / pornography (for pleasure and relief)
- Food (for relief from boredom; for health, pleasure, peace)
- Inheritance, insurance, possessions (for future security)
- My job (for security, status, financial gain)
- My kids, job, marriage (for happiness)
- Physical appearance (for fitness, beauty)
- My gifts / abilities

Do not turn away after useless idols. They can do you no good, nor can they rescue you, because they are worthless (I Samuel 12:20). The difference between trusting idols and trusting the true God is like the difference between drinking seawater and drinking fresh water. Two things happen when you drink seawater: you get even thirstier and you start to go crazy. Idolatry causes your view of reality to become warped. Something that seemed so wrong in the past is now acceptable. What is more, you are not satisfied. A false god is just that – *false*. It can only lie. It promises life, but instead brings death (From *Gospel Transformation Workbook*, pp. 45-46, 49).

God the Creator

In 2005, I spent a month in Shenyang, China. My wife and I were visiting our daughter who taught at an international school. During our stay, I taught *Business English* classes to Chinese adults at Northeastern University. The students asked me, "Where are you from? Where do you live?" They were familiar with the United States, but not Omaha, Nebraska.

Do you believe that you have a creator? Virtually every product has a label that identifies where it was made. Where did you come from? You came from God.

Our greatest need is not to find a religion or a set of ethics. Our greatest need is to know the God who made us. In the inspired Scriptures, God first reveals Himself as our Creator:

Genesis 1:1	In the beginning God *created* the heavens and the earth.
Genesis 1:28	So God *created* man in his own image, in the image of God he *created* him; male and female he *created* them.
Psalm 100:3	Know that the Lord is God. It is He who *made* us.
Acts 17:24-25	The God who *made* the world and everything in it is the Lord of heaven and earth and does not live in temples built by hands. And he is not served by human hands, as if he needed anything, because he himself gives all men life and breath and everything else.

The Image of God

There are only two categories of life in the universe: *uncreated* and *created*. God is *uncreated*. With no beginning or end, no past or future, God is eternal and unchanging.

People are in the category of *created life*. God created people to reflect His divine image. *Then God said, Let us make man in our image, in our likeness* (Genesis 1:26). No other part of creation enjoys this privilege. God did not create us in His own image so that we would merely have a sense of ethics. God created us to personally know Him. God wants an easy, uninhibited relationship with us. He wants a relationship that is restful and healing to our soul.

God loves us for ourselves. He values our love more than He values all the galaxies in the universe. *When God created man, he made him in the likeness of God. He created them male and female* (Genesis 5:1-2). Both men and women were created to enjoy a special relationship with God Himself.

Both Scripture and nature demonstrate the uniqueness of human beings. God views all people as responsible and accountable individuals because they possess personal freedom. Although the Bible never describes in detail what it means to be made in God's image, several implications are clear. People have the following characteristics:

RATIONAL	An intelligent mind with the capacity to reason, evaluate and even criticize themselves.
VOLITIONAL	The ability to make commitments; a free will to choose and decide.
RELATIONAL	Personal longings that include the desire to love and be loved.
CREATIVE	The capacity to design, build, organize and rule over creation.
MORAL	A conscience that enables them to recognize right and wrong and make moral choices.
SPIRITUAL	The inclination to worship, pray and relate to God.

PEOPLE MATTER

We matter to God. God made human beings to know Him, serve one another and manage the earth. This is the kind of dignity God granted people. Respect for God, others and yourself results from understanding what it means to be created in the image of God.

The hand of God leaves its imprint on all people. Everyone is made to reflect God's likeness. This is a unique privilege reserved for man alone. Every child has a father. Being created in God's image means **we have an identity** that flows from God – our heavenly Father. When our identity is rooted in God, we derive a sense of security and confidence.

Being created in God's image means **we have worth.** Human life is sacred. We are all connected because we have the same Creator. At their core, all people have the same needs, fears, desires and hopes. God has no favorites. He values all people equally.

Being created in God's image means **we have a built-in hunger for relationships.** None of us can go through life without the help of others. We are dependent on others for our very survival from the moment of conception. Furthermore, we come to discover who we are through our relationships. Marriage, family, friends and neighbors are just a few of the relationships that touch this deeply felt longing for love and acceptance.

Being created in God's image means **we possess a natural impulse to worship.** God created moral beings, spiritually and intellectually capable of worshiping Him. The one mark that distinguishes humans from all other forms of life on earth is that people have the inclination and capacity to worship.

True worship encompasses all of life. It is a lifestyle of dependence upon God for our daily existence. Our life is *derived from* and *dependent on* God. He is the source of our existence. No one is self-made and self-sufficient. Everything we need comes from the hand of God.

Worship is more than attending church services. Worship is the conscious awareness of God's presence. It is our personal friendship with a living God, moment by moment, day by day.

The spiritual elements of worship include: adoration, love, fascination, attachment and devotion. Worship is the way we express what we feel in our heart. It is not expressed in the same way all the time – but it is expressed.

Being created in God's image means **we know the reason for our existence.** One of the most searching questions is, "What is man's purpose?" The answer is to glorify God. *You are worthy, our Lord and God, to receive glory and honor and power, for you created all things, and by your will they were created and have their being* (Revelation 4:11).

In *The World's Challenge to the Church,* John Stott writes,

> Christian teaching on the dignity, nobility and worth of human beings is very important today. When human beings are devalued, everything in society goes sour: Women and children are despised. The sick are regarded as a nuisance and the elderly as a burden. Ethnic minorities are discriminated against. Capitalism displays its ugliest face. Labor is exploited in the mines and factories. Criminals are brutalized in prison. Human life seems not worth living because it is scarcely human any longer.
>
> But when human beings are valued because of their intrinsic worth, everything changes: Women and children are honored. The sick are cared for and the elderly are allowed to live and die with dignity. Prisoners are rehabilitated and minorities are protected. Workers are given a fair wage, decent work conditions and a measure of participation in the enterprise. Why? Because people matter. Every man, woman and child has significance as a person made in the image of God.

God is. God is here. God is here first.

God is real whether or not we acknowledge His existence. We all tend to lose sight of the fact that we are living our life in someone else's universe. This is God's universe, not ours. He made it and it belongs to him.

The single most important thing about us is our idea of God. What really comes to mind when you think about God? Do realize that a living and loving God is seeking you today?

We must guard ourselves from looking back at the past and seeing only the God who *was*. Likewise, we must avoid the habit of only looking forward and picturing the God who *will be*. To think of God only in terms of your past and your future, leaves Him absent in your present.

The one, true, living God is here right *now*. He is the same yesterday, today and forever. This is the God who is – the God of the Bible – and apart from Him there is no other.

The God who made you is on your side. He wants to help you. You will find God when you seek Him with all your heart. The end of your search is closer than you may think. If you are ready to discover how personal God can be, open your heart and pray. Ask God to reveal Himself today.

Individual Response Questions

1. When did you first recognize the possibility of a Creator God?

2. If God does exist, why does it matter that you believe in Him?

3. Which heart-idols have you observed? How do they begin to rule one's life?

4. What does it mean to be made in the image of God?

5. How does God's existence change the way we treat people?

6. What part of this lesson was most meaningful to you?

Personal Assessment

On a scale from 1-6, circle your response (1 means *not true* of you; 6 means *is true* of you).

- I believe that God exists.

  1 2 3 4 5 6

- I believe that there is only one God.

  1 2 3 4 5 6

- I recognize my heart-idols.

  1 2 3 4 5 6

- I know God created me in His image.

  1 2 3 4 5 6

- I believe that it is possible to have a relationship with God.

  1 2 3 4 5 6

Lesson 2 – Man as God Intended

§

Everything was Prepared

When I was thirteen years old, my brother and I rode the train from Denver to St. Louis to visit my grandmother. While there, she asked us if we would be interested in going to a St. Louis Cardinal's baseball game. The idea thrilled us! Then it got interesting.

Her next words were, "First, I need to pick up a friend of mine to go with us." On the way to the stadium we stopped by an apartment building and an 85-year-old woman joined my grandmother in the front seat.

As my brother and I sat quietly behind them, I began losing interest in this activity. I liked baseball, but the thought of spending the entire day with two old ladies was not appealing.

To my surprise, this day was nothing like I had imagined. My first clue that something was different was the fact that we drove directly to the front of the stadium. A man in a uniform approached our car, opened the door and said, "Good afternoon Mrs. Divine." He then helped us out of the car.

The next thing I remember is watching everyone standing in long ticket lines – everyone but us. We were ushered through a special door and another man in a uniform said, "Good afternoon Mrs. Divine."

While others were walking up multi-leveled ramps, we were taken to an exclusive elevator. The attendant said, "Good afternoon Mrs. Divine." Before I knew it, we were escorted to the private box of the General Manager of the St. Louis Cardinals. Clearly, we were not sitting with the "common peasant people."

Little did I realize, but the 85-year-old woman in our company was the mother of Bing Divine, the General Manager of the Cardinals. When you're the mother of the General Manager, it seems everyone associated with the organization knows your name. I was only thirteen years old, but people I had never met were awaiting my arrival. Total strangers opened doors for me. I received the privilege of watching the game in the comfort of the General Manager's private box.

It was not because of who I was, but rather who Mrs. Divine was. This kind, elderly woman made one phone call and everything was prepared. I did nothing to deserve it and had no means of repaying her generosity. It was a day I will never forget.

I can easily imagine that when God created the world, He looked forward to showing Adam and Eve the planet that He prepared. They received a perfect world, not because of who they were, but rather who God was. God wanted Adam and Eve to enjoy a world with no flaws or defects. There was nothing they could do to repay the Lord for His generosity. This was the way God intended it.

Regretfully, those days are gone. Today, neither the world nor mankind is what God intended. What happened? In the Scriptures, God tells us. The Bible reveals how God made us, what God originally intended and how our current fallen spiritual condition came to be.

People are Dependent

God made people. God knows people. Some believe that our only source of information about people is scientific experimentation, observation and speculation. Thankfully there is another source. **The most accurate source that can help us understand ourselves is the Bible.**

From the Bible, we learn that people are both *physical* and *spiritual*. The physical is the outward part. The spiritual is the inward part. If we knew how God intended us to function, we could better understand our spiritual condition today. When my daughter Crystal was in the fifth grade, her teacher asked her to write a paper entitled "My Personality." Here is an excerpt:

> My name is Crystal. I am ten years old. I was born May 30, 1980. My mom's name is Peggy, my dad's name is Paul and my sister's name is Carey. I have blue eyes and light brown hair. I am tall for my age and average for my weight. I am smart and go to a gifted class. I inherited a singing talent from my mother and my father, but I got my intelligence from my mom's side of the family.

Despite the questionable accuracy of her paper, Crystal somehow recognized that her gifts and abilities came from a source outside herself. God wants you to recognize that your spiritual life is dependent on an outside source. That source is God. This is not referring to His teaching, His example or His instruction – but rather *Himself*. God Himself always intended to live within us. To understand this truth, consider how human beings are designed.

Outward Part

God created all people with a physical dimension we refer to as the human body. Our bodies are the outward part of us created to give us a "house" to live in and a means of communication with the outside world. The human body is the physical, visible and tangible part of us, not the spiritual. It is the material part that we can touch. It has actual form and substance.

The reason God gave us a body is so that we could visibly reflect His likeness. People are created to function like a mirror. Just as a mirror reflects your likeness, God intends your actions to reflect His likeness (His character and heart). Our outward behavior can give a physical, visible and audible reflection of an invisible God.

Inward Part

There is more to us than our body. Our human body is not who we really are – it is merely the house we live in. Inside every human being is the life of the person. We naturally think of this inward dimension as our *self* or *personality.*

All people have an inward personality. The three basic aspects of our inner self are *thoughts, feelings* and *choices*. Under the influence of our mind and emotions, we have the capacity to make decisions and interact with others.

Deepest Part

The Bible teaches that we have another very unique dimension that goes even deeper than our thoughts and feelings. The deepest part of every human being is the *heart, soul, spirit* and *will*. The Bible calls this our *inner most being*. It is the executive center where all decisions and choices are ultimately made. The terms in Scripture that refer to our deepest nature seem to overlap and are often used interchangeably. Here are some examples:

Psalm 19:7-8	The law of the Lord is perfect, reviving the *soul*. The precepts of the Lord are right, giving joy to the *heart*.
Psalm 51:10	Create in me a pure *heart*...renew a steadfast *spirit* within me.
Psalm 103:1	Bless the Lord, my *soul;* all my *inmost being*, praise His holy name.
Mark 12:30	Love the Lord your God with all your *heart* and with all your *soul*...
Hebrews 4:12	The word of God is living and active; it penetrates even to dividing *soul* and *spirit;* it judges the thoughts and intentions of the *heart*.

God created all people with a physical and a spiritual dimension. While some may see themselves as a *body with a soul*, God sees us as a *soul with a body*. The essence of life is spiritual, not physical. To the question, "Who am I?" professor and author Dr. Dallas Willard offers this answer: *I am an unceasing spiritual being with an eternal destiny in God's great universe*.

God's Intention

Regardless of what we call the center or core of human life, the Bible declares that God intends to live there. We are created to be inhabited. Man is the dwelling place for God Himself.

From the first chapter of the Bible, we learn that God's plan was to make a creature called man that would reflect His perfect likeness. *Then God said, "Let us make man in our image, in our likeness"* (Genesis 1:26). To accomplish His purpose, God put His own Spirit within man. *And the Lord God formed man from the dust of the ground and breathed into his nostrils the breath of life, and man became a living being* (Genesis 2:7). In Scripture, the word for *breath* and *spirit* are the same. God's breath is His spiritual life and presence.

When God breathed into man *the breath of life,* His Holy Spirit came to dwell within him. God never intended man to live his life uninhabited. This simply means that the presence of the Holy Spirit within our human spirit is indispensable to our ability to function as God intended. Many Bible verses emphasize this reality:

Genesis 2:7	God formed man from the dust of the ground and *breathed* into his nostrils the *breath* of life.
Ezekiel 36:26-27	I will give you a new heart and put a new spirit in you. I will put my *Spirit* in you and move you to follow my decrees.
John 3:6, 8	Flesh gives birth to flesh, but the *Spirit* gives birth to *spirit*. The wind blows wherever it pleases. So it is with everyone born of the *Spirit*.
Romans 8:16	The *Spirit* himself testified with our *spirit* that we are God's children.
Galatians 4:6	Because you are sons, God sent the *Spirit* of his Son into our hearts.
Ephesians 3:16	I pray that He may strengthen you with power through *His Spirit* in your *inner being*.

The example of an *oil lamp* clearly illustrates this principle. An oil lamp is merely a container. The energy source for the flame is the oil *within* the lamp. The human spirit is merely the "lamp." God's Spirit is the "oil."

Consider how the moon reflects the light of the sun. The moon has no light in itself. The light it reflects comes from another source – the sun. Just as the moon cannot generate light by itself, man cannot generate God's likeness by himself.

Just as the moon is dependent upon a solar light source for its image, we are dependent on a divine life source to reflect God's image. We are dependent upon the indwelling presence of God's Spirit. God always intended to be the origin of His own image.

The Origin of Death

There is a big difference between what God had in mind when he created the world, and what we see today. Something happened between man and God, and between man and his fellow man. God expected man to remain faithful through his love for Him, dependence on Him and obedience to Him. If man ever adopted a self-sufficient attitude toward his Creator, *he would die*.

The Scriptures speak of death in three ways: *Physical Death* – the separation of the spirit from the body; *Spiritual Death* – the separation of the spirit from God; and *Eternal Death* – the separation of both spirit and body from God forever. **Because of sin, *death* is the best word that summarizes the human predicament.** Adam and Eve believed Satan's lies and disobeyed God's Word. Initially, they experienced *spiritual death*. In time they *died physically*.

When Adam and Eve sinned, God withdrew His Holy Spirit from their human spirit and they forfeited the life of God. They became uninhabited and separated from their only source of spiritual life. The physical removal of Adam and Eve from the Garden of Eden symbolizes the spiritual removal of God's Holy Spirit from their heart (Genesis 3:23 and Ephesians 4:18). Adam and Eve now had to make it on their own.

The Spread of Sin

Originally, God made man sinless. Today, man is fallen. Adam's sin has been passed down to the entire human race. *When Adam had lived 130 years, he had a son in his own likeness, in his own image* (Genesis 5:3). The world today is full of people who are created to reflect God's image, but like Adam, no longer accurately reflect His likeness.

The Bible calls this distortion *sin*. All people have sinned; it is a universal spiritual condition. Only Jesus is without sin. In essence, sin is any thought, word or action that falls short of reflecting God's likeness. Scripture describes sin several different ways:

- Failing to live up to God's standards
- Doing what is morally wrong by lying, cheating, stealing
- Perverting what is good
- Disregarding a known boundary and doing what is forbidden
- Neglecting to carry out clear instructions from God

Sin causes humans to live as if they are accountable to no one but themselves. Sin is the decision to live life away from God rather than toward Him. Sin is opposed to God. We sin when we do not submit to the rule of God. We sin when we place ourselves in charge of our lives.

God designed us to love Him first. Sin puts our will before God. The effect of sin is always negative. In addition to distorting the image of God, sin has other characteristics:

CONGENITAL	Sin is an inherited spiritual disease. We are born with its infection in our nature. It is present at birth.
ADDICTIVE	Sin is drug-like. It's easy to get hooked and hard to break free.
ALIENATING	Sin cuts us off from God and creates conflict with others.
DESTRUCTIVE	Sin destroys our conscience, self-worth and reputation.
ENSLAVING	Sin captures and imprisons. 'Slave' describes many people.

Sin is like putting your hand in a bucket of glue and then trying to wipe it clean. Everything you touch becomes sticky and there's nowhere to wash it off. Adam's sin began a cycle that eventually touched every person on earth, just as a damaged cookie cutter would affect an entire batch of cookies. A dent in a cookie cutter would appear in any cookie it made. Adam is the original human cookie cutter and the "dent" of sin has been passed down ever since.

Sin has created an unloving world. We all share some responsibility for the sin that is in the world today. The solution for our condition is to discover a way to deal with sin and get God back into our life. Thankfully, God loved us and sent His Son Jesus to provide us with such a solution through His Son, Jesus.

Jesus Christ died for our sins. Jesus rose from the dead. Jesus has the power to live in us again through the Person of the Holy Spirit. Today, Satan continues to deceive people into thinking that they can make it on their own. We need God living within us to fulfill our created purpose.

What God is Like

Major Ian Thomas told a story that is full of imaginary characters, but it has a powerful message:

> On an imaginary planet lived some imaginary creatures. The same God who made you and me made these creatures. But unlike us they didn't know what God was like.
>
> One day these creatures learned that far out into space there was another planet called Earth. On planet Earth, God made a creature called man who reflected His perfect image. God did this so that all creation looking at man would know what God was like.
>
> They thought if only they could get to Earth, they too would know what God was like. They mobilized their resources, built a spaceship and chose a delegation for this important mission. After an official farewell they began their long journey.
>
> When their spaceship reached its destination their hearts raced with excitement. They said to one another, "We're about to step out onto a planet called Earth. In just a few moments we will see a creature called man that God made in His perfect image. The moment we see *man* we'll know what God is like. Once we know, we'll return home and tell our fellow creatures."
>
> When they stepped out of their spaceship and began to look around they were shocked beyond belief. They saw men lying face down in the streets, drunk with alcohol and addicted to drugs.
>
> They discovered wars, senseless bombings and world violence. They caught a glimpse of man's concept of pleasure, competition and entertainment. They noticed man's tendency to lie, cheat and deal corruptly in business.
>
> They detected man's tendency to love things and use people. They witnessed those who were consumed with sex, money and power. They viewed broken families and the pain that resulted. They saw a world where anything goes.

> After a while they couldn't stand it anymore and said, "Let's get out of here!" Sadly they began the long journey back to their own planet. A great crowd had gathered to give them a glorious welcome.
>
> As they stepped out of their spaceship, their fellow creatures immediately sensed that something was wrong. The throng became deathly quiet. The leader of the delegation broke the silence.
>
> "Fellow creatures, we have some bad news for you. We have been to Earth and have seen a creature called man, made in God's image, and now we know what God is like. God is a drunk, a murderer and a liar. God is selfish and self-centered. God is hurtful, hateful and vengeful. God is full of lust, envy and greed. We have seen *man* – and now we know what God is like."

Unfortunately, they didn't find out what God was like – they found out what sin was like. They didn't find man as God intended, they found man as he is today – spiritually dead and without God in his heart. They found people who had lost God somewhere along the way. They discovered men and women trying to make it on their own.

The Truth About People

Nero was the emperor of Rome from AD 54-68. The youthful Nero held great promise. He was gifted in poetry and music. He ruled with kindness and moderation. He only inflicted the death penalty in extreme cases. His teachers described him as a wise and just leader. They thought he was incapable of learning cruelty. They believed the emperor's gentle disposition would transform the world and restore the innocent, golden age of mankind. Then something happened.

Within a few years of becoming emperor, Nero degenerated into a person who enjoyed getting pleasure from mistreating others. As a leader he began to demand public praise as a god. He ordered the murder of his brother, mother and first wife. His second wife died from personal abuse. His most tragic act was setting fire to the city of Rome and then blaming the followers of Jesus for the crime. He is remembered as a horrible monster.

Like Nero, all people have the capacity to do good *and* evil. Sometimes we are kind, loving and helpful; other times we are mean, hateful and cruel. Sometimes we choose to be selfish rather than to share. Sometimes we decide to exert power over people rather than to serve them. God is always good. Sin is always wrong. What do your actions reflect? Are you living as God intended?

Individual Response Questions

1. Why must God inhabit a person in order for His likeness to be reflected?

2. Which Bible verses regarding God indwelling us did you find most significant? Why?

3. If the inner person is so important, why do people focus so much on outward appearance?

4. Which devastating characteristic of sin have you personally observed?

5. Without God, why can't people make it by themselves?

6. What part of this lesson was most meaningful to you?

Personal Assessment

On a scale from 1-6 circle your response (1 means *not true* of you; 6 means *is true* of you).

- I am actively trying to reflect God by my behavior.

  1 2 3 4 5 6

- I consistently think of myself as a soul with a body.

  1 2 3 4 5 6

- I readily give God credit as being the source of my spiritual life.

  1 2 3 4 5 6

- I am aware of the times I try to make it on my own.

  1 2 3 4 5 6

- I readily identify my sins.

  1 2 3 4 5 6

Lesson 3 – The One Who's Missing

§

The Need for God

In his book, *The Lotus and the Cross,* Ravi Zacharias tells of a woman from Bangkok, Thailand. A newspaper article reported this story of a young, attractive woman who left home at the age of seventeen to earn a better living.

Within hours of reaching Bangkok, the very friend who enticed her with the promise of big money, mercilessly raped her. To mend her torn spirit, her "friend" found her a job as a seamstress. But those associates turned ugly and soon afterward she was used and abused. By the age of twenty-three she had become a full-fledged prostitute.

Once, she found herself pregnant. She put her profession on hold for a few months until she could have the baby – only to give it away. The financial strain pressured her to return to the life that enslaved her. The most devastating shock came when she discovered she was HIV-positive.

She couldn't discontinue her lifestyle because she needed the money. By now she was hardened and vengeful. She continued to sell her services to hundreds of customers. She knew she was signing each man's death warrant, but she was drowning in despair and her life had lost all value.

Eventually she could no longer hide the disfiguring marks of her disease. Blisters blanketed her body. The desperate methods she tried in search for a cure had failed. She decided to kill herself numerous times, only to fail each time.

Finally, she poisoned herself once more and this time set her house on fire. Her once beautiful body was now ashes. No one came close to her charred remains for fear of infection. She died alone. Not far away, others played the same deadly game.

Like you, this woman was created in the image of God. She sought fulfillment but didn't find it. She died feeling rejected, betrayed and abandoned. What was missing? Surely this is not what God intended.

What's Missing?

When people are born, something is missing. More accurately, *someone* is missing. Initially, people do not recognize that Jesus is the person who is missing. Some people hold the view that God is for the weak. In other words, if your life is a mess and you can't make it on your own, then God may be your answer.

A Chinese man told me that as a youth, his instructors dismissed the notion that God could save him. They repeatedly emphasized that you can't expect God to save you – you must save yourself. The reality is people have been trying to do just that for thousands of years.

Regardless of who you are or where you are from, you need God in your life. Many people look for substitutes that can take the place of God and fill the emptiness of their heart. Some look to family, money and possessions. Others look to work, success and recognition. Have you come to the point where you recognize your need for God? Some people have – many haven't.

Well known, Yet Not Followed

Jesus is perhaps the most well known person in history. Even those who would never claim to be religious are familiar with the name *Jesus*. Many people alive today have seen a movie about the life and teachings of Jesus.

In 1979, The *Jesus* film was released. Since then, the cumulative worldwide viewing audience of the *Jesus* film is more than 6 billion. It has been shown in over 200 countries and translated into more than 1,000 different languages.

More recently, Academy Award winning actor and director Mel Gibson co-wrote, directed, produced, and financed *The Passion of the Christ*. The film was released on March 11, 2004. Millions of people saw this film. It graphically portrays the reason Jesus came to earth – to die on a cross for the sins of the world.

By Labor Day 2004, the film earned $370 million in the U.S. and Canada and over $600 million worldwide. In the United States, it is one of the highest grossing films of all time. This kind of exposure makes you wonder why more people don't believe in Jesus.

What others think of Jesus doesn't matter – it only matters what you think. Nothing keeps people away from Jesus more than their inability to see or admit their need. Consider your own attitude. Right now, do you need Jesus in your life?

Jesus said, *It is not the healthy who need a doctor, but the sick. I have not come to call the righteous, but sinners* (Mark 2:17). Jesus is not teaching that some people are so *healthy* that they don't need salvation. Rather, He is emphasizing that some people *think* they are healthy and thus never come to Him.

Do You Need Him?

In the summer of 2005, I was walking through the parking garage at my office. On the concrete floor was some water I didn't see. I accidentally slipped, fell on my left side and landed on a five-gallon metal can. It knocked the wind out of me. I was sore enough to go the doctor and get some x-rays. The diagnosis was two fractured ribs. I received some pain pills and the encouragement to take it easy for the next six weeks.

It took more than an accident accompanied by severe pain to get me to go to the doctor. I had to admit that I needed help. Just as we go to the doctor *only when* we admit that we are ill and cannot cure ourselves, so we will come to Christ only when we admit our need for Him. Deny the problem and nothing can be done – admit the problem and there is hope. Spiritually, self-salvation is impossible.

As the Great Physician, Jesus compares our spiritual condition to a physical disability. He came to heal those who were blind to God's truth and deaf to God's voice. Ironically, the religious leaders in Jesus' day needed Him most. He called them blind guides (Matthew 23:16, 24).

Jesus wants to give us His healing touch, but He won't force His way into our lives. If we never face up to the seriousness of our illness, we will never admit our urgent need for a cure. Opening up to Jesus takes time. Initially, we all have questions about who Jesus really is. If that is you, consider praying this prayer: ***Father in heaven, show me what Jesus has to do with me.***

WHO IS JESUS CHRIST?

If you find it difficult to believe in God, consider a different approach. Don't begin your search with philosophical questions – begin with Jesus of Nazareth. If you read the biblical story as an honest and humble seeker, Jesus Christ will reveal Himself to you. In the process of learning about Jesus, God the Father will become real also.

Jesus is the central figure of the Bible. The name Jesus means *savior* and His title, Christ, means *anointed*. Jesus is God's Son, sent from heaven to earth to die for the sins of all people.

He was born in Bethlehem, about five miles south of Jerusalem. He was raised in a Jewish family in the town of Nazareth. Through His love for God, dependence on God and obedience to God, Jesus did what no one else has ever done – He lived a sinless life.

Around age thirty-three, following a three-year ministry of teaching and healing, Jewish religious leaders falsely accused him. They handed him over to the Romans, who occupied Israel, to be executed. He was crucified on a cross, buried, rose from the dead and ascended back to heaven.

Four historical sources (Matthew, Mark, Luke and John) record many events from His life, including His miracles and sermons. Let Jesus introduce Himself to you in His own words:

John 6:51	I am the living bread that came down from heaven.
John 8:12	I am the light of the world.
John 8:58	I tell you the truth, before Abraham was born, I am.
John 10:9	I am the gate. Whoever enters through me will be saved.
John 10:10	I am the good shepherd. The good shepherd lays down his life for the sheep.
John 11:25	I am the resurrection and the life.
John 14:6	I am the way and the truth and the life. No one comes to the Father except through me.
John 15:5	I am the vine; you are the branches. If a man remains in me and I in him, he will bear much fruit; apart from me you can do nothing.

The Gospel – A Message of Hope

Jesus is the most important person we can ever know. He wants us to understand His message, receive His love and experience His life. *Gospel,* is the word God uses in the Bible to announce His completed plan to save the world. The gospel is not good advice to men, but good news about Christ. It is the message of what God has done for all people through His Son, Jesus. Stated simply, the message is this: **Christ died for our sins and was raised from the dead.**

The foundation of Christianity is Jesus Himself. Christianity is not a set of ethics to be debated and discussed. It is not a religion of rules – it is a message of hope. It is not a demand, but a gift. The gospel is an invitation to have a relationship with Jesus – to find forgiveness for your past and hope for your future.

The good news began with Jesus' birth. Though historians do not know the exact day, December 25th (Christmas) was designated to mark the birth of Jesus into the world. Jesus was born approximately 2,000 years ago. His entrance into the world was miraculous. A miracle is something that cannot be explained apart from God. Miracles are supernatural.

People perform magic – only God performs miracles. A young virgin named Mary was chosen by God to give birth to Jesus. She was not married and had never had sexual relations. By God's Spirit, Jesus came from heaven – to earth – through Mary. This was no ordinary baby.

His birth altered history so dramatically that our modern dating system is rooted in Jesus Christ. Years before the birth of Christ are designated **BC** – *Before Christ*. Years after His birth are designated **AD** – *Anno Domini* – which means: "In the Year of our Lord." (From *anno,* comes the word *annual;* from *domini,* comes the word *dominion.*)

The initial focal point of the gospel is Jesus' death on the cross. Jesus died to redeem us from sin. *Redeem* means to set someone free by making a ransom payment. In the first century, prisoners and slaves could be redeemed, or set free only when a ransom payment was made on their behalf. *The Son of Man did not come to be served, but to serve, and give his life as a ransom for many* (Mark 10:45). *Our redemption is through His blood* (Ephesians 1:7).

The price God accepted to set us free was the blood of Jesus. Jesus died because we could not redeem ourselves. **Jesus paid a debt He did not owe to give us a gift we could not buy.**

The ultimate focal point of the gospel is Jesus' resurrection. How do we know that Jesus is really who He claimed to be? How can we know that the Spirit of another Person can actually live within us? The answer is: **the resurrection**.

The resurrection from the dead is the foundational event for all of Jesus' teachings. The resurrection refers to Jesus' rising again from the dead three days after His burial. His burial followed his death on the cross. His death by crucifixion took place in Jerusalem in AD 30, immediately before the Jewish Passover.

The meaning of the resurrection is that Jesus lives. On Easter Sunday, followers of Jesus reaffirm their belief that Jesus was raised from the dead. Easter is celebrated on Sunday, since it was on this day that Jesus rose from the dead and was seen by His disciples (Matthew 28:1-20).

The date of Easter is set in relation to the same natural signs that mark the celebration of the Jewish Passover. It is generally observed on the first Sunday after the first full moon that occurs on or after March 21.

Apart from this foundational truth, following Jesus is meaningless. Jesus truly rose from the dead. Jesus did not merely resuscitate. He did not revive from a coma. The historical record is clear. He suffered on the cross and when examined, was pronounced dead. He was speared in His side and both blood and water gushed forth, indicating a ruptured pericardium (the sac around the heart).

Those who examined Him waived the Roman practice of breaking the legs because He was obviously dead. Jesus was a corpse taken from the cross and buried in a tomb cut out of a rock. Pilate ordered the tomb to be sealed and a Roman guard was set to ensure against grave theft (Matthew 27:62-66).

On the third day following His burial, Jesus rose again according to His own prophecies that death could not bind Him. This historic narrative may be read in the New Testament Gospels: Matthew 28, Mark 16, Luke 24 and John 20 - 21.

The New Testament records no less than a dozen instances of people witnessing the resurrected Christ on earth following His resurrection. For forty days, as few as two and as many as five hundred, ate with Him and touched Him (John 20:14-31).

Over the centuries, skeptics and doubters have earnestly searched to disprove the historical resurrection of Jesus because they know that all vital faith rests on this historic phenomenon. If it can be disproved, the teachings of Jesus would mean nothing.

However, the truth of Jesus' resurrection has stood the test of time. Millions have had life-changing encounters with the person of Jesus. Followers of Jesus personally experience the presence and power of Jesus for one simple reason – He physically rose from the dead.

It is the certainty of Jesus' resurrection that gives us inner strength for the present and the future. Followers of Jesus believe in life after death because of His resurrection. Jesus assured His followers, *because I live, you shall live too* (John 14:19). The life of Christ within us provides the power we need to fulfill our purpose on earth. He will lead us into the tomorrows of the next week, not just the tomorrows of the next life.

The birth, life, death and resurrection of Jesus are the good news of the gospel. Many people mistakenly conclude that the only reason to believe in Jesus is to go to heaven and avoid going to hell when they die. (Hell is a place of punishment for unbelievers.) The good news is that God wants to change your life *now.*

The goal of the gospel is not just to get you out of hell and into heaven – but to get God out of heaven and back into you. Through Jesus, God's plan is to restore to you the spiritual life that Adam lost in the Garden of Eden. Jesus died to forgive you and rose from the dead to live in you. That's the message of the gospel.

Eternal Life

Many people assume that eternal life begins at death. As a result, they only associate eternal life with heaven. It is true that followers of Jesus are promised that they will live with God in heaven for eternity. However, eternal life is also something Jesus gives his followers *today.*

Jesus said, *I am the life* (John 14:6). This means that eternal life is a **person,** not just a destination. The Scriptures teach that eternal life is a new quality of life that you experience by knowing Jesus. It begins on earth and continues in heaven. The apostle John (one of Jesus' twelve chosen followers) wrote that eternal life is experienced *now* by believing and following Jesus. Many Bible verses teach this spiritual reality:

John 3:36	Whoever believes in the Son has eternal life.
John 5:24	Whoever hears my word and believes Him who sent me has eternal life and will not be condemned; he has crossed over from death to life.
John 10:10	I have come that they may have life and have it more abundantly.
John 17:3	This is eternal life: that they may know you, the only true God and Jesus Christ whom you sent.
I John 5:11	God has given us eternal life, and this life is in his Son. He who has the Son has life; he who does not have the Son does not have life.

The Visitor

In his book, *The Divine Visitor,* Jack Hayford tells the story about a serviceman named Adam who was deployed to Iraq. After a year, when his leave finally approached, Adam called his parents and alerted them of his plans to come home. He didn't tell them the exact day because he wanted to surprise them.

Since his family lived on a farm many miles from a major city, getting home required Adam to take a series of buses and then walk the final fifteen miles to his parents' small Kansas farm.

He finally came to the long gravel road that led up to the old farmhouse. He had traveled all night and the sun was beginning to come up. Adam's little sister saw him first, but he motioned for her to keep quiet so that he could surprise the rest of the family. He made some coffee and waited for the fresh-brewed smell to permeate the house. His middle-age parents walked into the kitchen, wondering what was going on.

When they saw their son, tears of joy soon replaced the screams of surprise. The much-anticipated visitor had finally arrived. Few things are as wonderful as a visit from someone we dearly long to see. Hayford writes,

> What if you were summoned by God to visit a planet to help its deceived and corrupted inhabitants regain their lost nobility? To do so, you would have to become one of them. And yet you would be in constant danger. They would misunderstand your intentions. Many would hate and eventually kill you.

Knowing all this, would you still be willing to go to rescue any who might accept your intervening efforts? Would you relinquish the joys and securities of a vastly advantaged circumstance so that some might be recovered by your visit?

It has been done...by One whose love we cannot imagine. One *Visitor* in the past introduces the present promise of His ready availability to make a personal visit to you today.

In Jesus, God became a Visitor to mankind. With even more love for His creation than the homebound soldier had for his family, the Creator attests to the worth of His creation.

This is why He was willing to pay so exorbitant a price to regain mankind. We have been visited. And what's more He has also promised to stay with us forever – never leaving us, never forsaking us.

Jesus Christ is not just a crutch for the weak or an inspirational figure to help people find strength during hard times. He is not a fable, a myth or folklore. Jesus is not a subject you study – He is a person you experience. Jesus died *for you,* in order to live *in you*. That is very good news!

Individual Response Questions

1. How would Jesus have made a difference to the young woman from Thailand?

2. Which verse about Jesus' description of Himself do you find most encouraging?

3. Why is the resurrection of Jesus so important? What if Jesus hadn't risen from the dead?

4. What is eternal life? How do the verses describing eternal life alter the way you think of it?

5. What spiritual concept would you like to further explore?

6. What part of this lesson was most meaningful to you?

Personal Assessment

On a scale from 1-6 circle your response (1 means *not true* of you; 6 means *is true* of you).

- I daily recognize my need for Jesus.

  1 2 3 4 5 6

- I know how Jesus' death and resurrection can change my life.

  1 2 3 4 5 6

- The Gospel is clear to me. I understand it and am ready to explain it.

  1 2 3 4 5 6

- Eternal life is the life of Jesus living in my heart. I experience this new life daily.

  1 2 3 4 5 6

- I recognize that when Jesus came to Earth, God personally visited *me*.

  1 2 3 4 5 6

Lesson 4 – Your Second Chance

§

Starting Life Over

Ray Stedman told the story about a man who had been an alcoholic for many years before he became a follower of Jesus. One day a cynical friend asked him, "Now that you are a follower of Jesus, surely you don't believe all those miracles in the Bible, do you?"

"Yes I do," he answered.

After a moment of silence the skeptical friend said, "Do you really believe that Jesus changed water into wine?" "I sure do," the new believer said.

"But how can you believe such nonsense?"

"I'll tell you how – in our house Jesus changed beer into furniture!"

When Jesus comes into your heart, it isn't always sensational. It isn't always dramatic, but it is always a miracle. You know that you are not the same person you were before. It's like starting life over. Jesus said that everyone must have a fresh start. He called it being *born again*.

Being born again is a spiritual new birth. The biblical term for this miracle is *regeneration*. Regeneration means to begin again or start over. A person is regenerated when he receives God's Spirit. We are not only redeemed by God's Son, we are regenerated by God's Spirit. God made it possible to *begin again* because Jesus rose from the dead.

Once Born and Twice Born

A.W. Tozer wrote,

> Classification can be one of the most difficult tasks. But there is one distinction that we must make if we are to think like God and bring our thoughts in harmony with the Holy Scriptures. That distinction is the one which exists between two classes of human beings: the once-born and the twice-born.

Jesus said, *You must be born again. That which is born of flesh is flesh; and that which is born of Spirit is spirit* (John 3:3, 6). This clear line of separation runs through the entire New Testament. There is frankly no sharper distinction that more literally divides one human being from another than this. The presence of the Holy Spirit within the human spirit distinguishes a twice-born person from a once-born person.

We are wise if we honestly recognize that two human races occupy the earth simultaneously. One is a fallen race that originates from Adam. The other is a forgiven people who have been born again by personally trusting in Jesus. Twice-born people know Jesus personally. Once-born people may have heard about Jesus, but don't know Him.

All people are made in God's image, but not everyone has a relationship with Jesus. Some people are once-born, others are twice-born. Being twice-born does not make you better than others, just different. The twice-born person is the temple of the Holy Spirit. God lives in him. The once-born person has not received the Spirit of God because he has not trusted Jesus as his Savior. The indwelling presence of Jesus is the test that determines whether you have been born again. Look at what the Bible says about spiritual new birth:

John 1:12	To those who receive Him, who believe in His name, He gave the right to become children of God – children *born* not of natural descent, nor of a human decision or a husband's will, but *born* of God.
John 3:6	Flesh gives birth to flesh, but Spirit gives birth to spirit. You should not be surprised at my saying, "You must be *born again*."
I Peter 1:3	God has given us *new birth* into a living hope through the resurrection of Jesus Christ.
I John 5:1	Everyone who believes that Jesus is the Christ is *born* of God.

A Personal Experience

In the Bible, being born again is experiencing God's salvation. Salvation is a personal miracle. It is personal because it is between you and the Lord. It is a miracle because salvation is God's work in your heart made possible by God's work on the cross. Salvation is miraculous because it requires as much power to save a soul as it does to raise the dead or open blind eyes.

When a man or woman becomes a follower of Jesus he or she is "saved." Jesus saved Zacchaeus, a dishonest tax collector. When Zacchaeus opened his heart and confessed his sins, Jesus said to him, *Today salvation has come to this house, for the Son of Man came to seek and to save what was lost* (Luke 19:9-10; *Son of Man* is a title Jesus often used to describe himself). Jesus pronounced Zacchaeus "saved." No man can forgive his own sins and save himself.

Before we can be saved, there is a condition that must be present in our hearts. Jesus said, *The time has come. The kingdom of God is near. Repent and believe the good news* (Mark 1:15). Jesus has made the kingdom of God fully accessible. Now it's our move.

A genuine salvation experience always begins with a pierced heart – a pricked conscience that is sensitive toward God. Repentance is a change of heart. To *repent* means to change your whole way of thinking. It is the willingness to turn around and go in a new direction. This "about face" flows from a conscious awareness of your need for God.

Next, is placing your faith in Jesus. A person isn't saved by religious education, merely reciting a prayer, or associating with church people. God wants us to trust and obey Jesus from our heart. This is very important because Jesus will not repent or believe *for us*. It is morally impossible for one person to respond for another. Christ's part was to die for us. Our part is to open our hearts and receive His free gift. Following Jesus is a personal choice. Each person deals directly with God. There are five personal miracles that lay the foundation for a changed life. Each miracle is an undeserved, permanent and irreversible gift from God. The five miracles are:

Total Forgiveness

The first miracle is an undeserved pardon based on Jesus' death. A follower of Jesus is forgiven of all sins – past, present and future. *In him (Jesus) we have redemption through his blood, the forgiveness of sins, in accordance with the riches of God's grace* (Ephesians 1:7). The death of Jesus cancelled our debt. It was a blood transaction – Jesus' blood for our freedom. This is the gift of God's grace, not something we earn or deserve. Jesus frees us to live for Him.

New Family

The second miracle is being adopted into God's family, the church. The church is also called Christ's body on earth. The Lord adds every follower of Jesus to His church. We belong to Jesus and others. We are members of God's spiritual family. *You are no longer foreigners and aliens, but fellow citizens with God's people and members of God's household* (Ephesians 2:19). We're adopted sons and daughters.

Spiritual Birth

The third miracle is receiving God's Spirit. The church began on the Day of Pentecost (fifty days after the Jewish Passover and ten days after Jesus ascended to heaven). On the Day of Pentecost, God poured out His Spirit on those who believed in Jesus.

The Scriptures promise each believer *the gift of the Holy Spirit* (Acts 2:38). Through the Holy Spirit, God marks us as His child. *Having believed, you were marked in him with a seal, the promised Holy Spirit* (Ephesians 1:13). By the Holy Spirit, we are born again – born from above.

Personal Destiny

The fourth miracle involves God's providential plan for your life. We are all created for a reason. For every member of the body of Christ, God has a purpose, a plan and a place. *For we are God's workmanship, created in Christ Jesus to do good works, which God prepared in advance for us to do* (Ephesians 2:10).

God determined the period in history in which you would live. God decided when and where you would be born. He knew you would read this workbook. God has an assignment just for you because none of us is the leading character in the story of our life.

Future Hope

The fifth miracle pertains to life after death. Jesus promises a home in heaven to all who believe in Him. When the thief who died next to Jesus expressed his faith, Jesus promised him, *Today you will be with me in paradise* (Luke 23:43).

The Scriptures assure us that the Lord knows who are His (II Timothy 2:19) and the names of God's people are recorded in the book of life (Philippians 4:3).

The Toughest Question

Jack Welch, the retired CEO of General Electric, is one of the most successful corporate executives in the history of American business. He is obsessed with being number one and *Winning*, is the title of one of his books.

Over his career, Jack has been criticized for firing too many people, being greedy and beginning a romantic relationship with a younger woman, Suzy Wetlaufer (24 years younger than Jack), while he was still married. She has since become the third Mrs. Jack Welch.

On March 30, 2005 during CBS' television program *60 Minutes*, Welch sat down with correspondent Dan Rather to set the record straight. At the very end of the interview, Dan asked Jack, "What's the toughest question you have ever been asked?" **"Do you think you'll go to heaven?"** said Welch. "Your answer?" asked Rather. Welch replied,

> It's a long answer, but I said that, if caring about people, if giving it your all, if being a great friend counts, despite the fact that I've been divorced a couple of times – and no one's proud of that – I haven't done everything right all the time, but I think I got a shot. I'm in no hurry to get there or to find out anytime soon.

Jack Welch's answer is very common. Many people envision the criterion for getting into heaven that of a giant scale where God weighs our good deeds and compares them to our bad deeds.

God is not keeping track of all of our actions to determine if we have done more good than bad. He promised all people that they will be welcomed into heaven based on their faith in Jesus. He knows that trying to be "good enough" is an impossible requirement. What if you were one good deed short? How would you know? You can't know and thankfully, God doesn't approach entrance into heaven on a **performance basis.**

When we stand before God, the most important question will not be, "Do you think you have done enough to get into heaven?" Jesus said, *Whoever acknowledges me before men, I will also acknowledge him before my Father in heaven* (Matthew 10:32).

The most important discussion will take place between God and Jesus. On that day, God will ask His Son, "Do you know this person?" Because of our trust in Him, Jesus will look at His Father and say, "Yes, he's with Me." When we admit to knowing Jesus on earth, Jesus will admit to knowing us in heaven. It's not about our performance – it's about our relationship with Jesus.

Jesus is Knocking

Regardless of our nationality, background or upbringing, none of us are "born" a Christian. To become a follower of Jesus requires a decisive act of trust. Each of us must decide for ourselves whether we are *for* or *against* Christ. Remaining neutral is not an option.

Following Jesus is deeper than *agreeing* with religious ideas. It is more than agreeing that Jesus is God's Son who died on a cross. It is more than agreeing that we are all sinners and in need of a Savior. There's more to it than agreeing to go to church and trying to be a decent person. Jesus wants a receptive heart that leads to a personal relationship.

In 1853, William Holman Hunt created his best-known painting, *The Light of the World*. It is a picture of Jesus (as the light of the world) knocking on a door with His right hand, while holding a lantern in His left. This painting is based on the words of Jesus:

> *Here I am! I stand at the door and knock. If anyone hears my voice and opens the door, I will come in and eat with him, and he with me.* (Revelation 3:20)

The door represents your heart. By knocking, Jesus is waiting for you to open the door of your life and invite Him in. He is standing at the door, not pushing. He could command you to open the door but leaves that decision up to you.

Why does He want to come into your heart? Jesus wants to come in to forgive your past and guide your future. He wants to come in so that you don't have to face your present circumstances alone. So what is Jesus waiting for? He's waiting for you to hear His voice and open the door.

The Skeptic

Lee Strobel was educated at Yale Law School. He was an award-winning legal editor of the *Chicago Tribune* and a spiritual skeptic until 1981. His book, *The Case for Easter,* probes the core issues of the resurrection of Jesus Christ from the dead.

When his own wife became a follower of Jesus, Lee decided to use his journalistic training to prove once and for all that Jesus was a fake. He believed that followers of Jesus were blinded to the real facts about Christ and saw only what they wanted to see. He once said, "As a reporter, I have seen lots of dead people – and none of them ever came back to life. People can spin fanciful tales of an empty tomb, but they could never change the grim, absolute finality of death."

Lee began his search for truth as an atheist. He interviewed experts in the fields of medicine, history and science. The testimony of medical doctors, scientists and professors finally led him to reach a verdict he never thought he could admit – **Jesus really is the Son of God.** Strobel writes,

> On November 8, 1981, I talked with God in a heart-felt and unedited prayer, admitting and turning from all my wrong-doing, and receiving the free gift of forgiveness and eternal life through Jesus. I told God that with His help I wanted to follow Him and His ways as best I could from that moment forward. Looking back, I can see that this was nothing less than the pivotal event of my entire life.
>
> Over time, my character, values, worldview, philosophy and relationships began to change – for the good. So much so, that a few months after I became a follower of Jesus, our five year-old daughter, Alison – who had previously only known a father who had been profane, angry, verbally harsh, drunken and all too often absent – walked up to my wife and said, "Mommy, I want God to do for me what He's done for Daddy."

Even at an early age, a five year-old child could see that her father found the person he was missing. Jesus is knocking. Are you ready to open the door?

The Iranian Student

In his book, *The Cross of Christ*, John Stott writes,

> *Irresistible* is the word an Iranian student used when telling me of his conversion to Christ. Brought up to read the Qur'an, say his prayers and lead a good life, he nevertheless knew that he was separated from God by his sins.
>
> When Christian friends brought him to church and encouraged him to read the Bible, he learned that Jesus Christ had died for his forgiveness. "For me, the offer was irresistible and heaven-sent," he said, and he cried to God to have mercy on him through Christ.
>
> "Almost immediately," he continued, "the burdens of my past life were lifted. I felt as if a huge weight had gone. With the relief and a sense of lightness came incredible joy. At last it had happened. I was free from my past. I knew that God had forgiven me and I felt clean. I wanted to shout and tell everybody."

It was through the cross and the character of God that he found Islam's missing dimension – the intimate fatherhood of God and the deep assurance of sins forgiven. **Jesus does not care about your past, your nationality or your former beliefs.** He is ready to accept any person and forgive any sin that is confessed. Jesus is knocking. Are you ready to open the door?

The Indian

In his book, *The Holy Spirit – Power from on High,* A. B. Simpson tells the story about an American Indian who was asked to share how he found God. When asked, the Indian initially said nothing. Instead he knelt down, found a little worm and put it on the ground.

The crowd watched him form a ring of dry leaves, put the worm in the middle, and build a fire around it. The fire surrounded the worm. The worm caught the smell of the fire, felt the dangerous heat and began to flee.

As the worm squirmed away from the flame, it quickly met another wall of fire on the other side. Everyone watched as the worm went back and forth from side to side in terror and despair.

Finally, the little worm, finding no way of escape, gathered itself up in the center of the circle and lay there helpless and dying. A concerned look came over the faces of those who were watching.

Then the Indian stretched out his hand, picked up the worm and saved it. He turned to the crowd and said, **"That is the way I was saved. It was by God's mercy."**

Have you ever felt like the little worm – frightened and trapped with no place to turn? In your lowest moment, God can rescue you too. Jesus is knocking. Are you ready to open the door?

Which Thief are You?

All four gospels confirm that Jesus was crucified between two thieves. One robber was on His right and the other was on His left (Matthew 27:38; Mark 15:27; Luke 23:33; John 19:33). Initially, both criminals mocked Jesus. While hanging on his cross, one of the robbers had a change of heart. Luke records the episode with these words:

> *One of the criminals who hung there hurled insults at him: "Aren't you the Christ? Save yourself and us!" But the other criminal rebuked him. "Don't you fear God," he said, "since you are under the same sentence? We are punished justly, for we are getting what our deeds deserve. But this man has done nothing wrong." Then he said, "Jesus, remember me when you come into your kingdom." Jesus answered him, "I tell you the truth, today you will be with me in paradise"* (Luke 23:39-42).

As Jesus hung on the cross, no one in history had a better view of His compassion and suffering than these two criminals. Both men heard what the angry crowd thought of Jesus. Both men watched Jesus extend forgiveness to Roman soldiers. Both men were able to speak directly to Jesus during their final hours on earth.

In the midst of this chaos, somehow the second thief came to terms with his personal failure, the punishment he deserved, and the reality that he was not ready to die. He courageously ignored the response of others and opened his heart to Jesus. With his last ounce of strength, he confessed his sin, affirmed Jesus' innocence and humbly asked Jesus to remember him in the future.

Jesus saved this broken man immediately and completely – by grace. The thief didn't deserve it and there was no time to earn it. His salvation was personally guaranteed by a simple promise – *"today you will be with me in paradise."*

It is easy to see three striking differences between these two men: One thief recognized his need for Jesus, the other didn't. One thief looked to Jesus for help, the other didn't. One thief received an eternal reward, the other didn't.

We are all like these two thieves – we've all done things we regret. The personal question for us is, **"Which thief are you?"** Are you the one that ridiculed – or the one that sought God's mercy?

Is today your day of salvation? Respond to His voice right now. God Himself has brought you to this moment. Open the door of your heart and ask Jesus to come in. Everyone who calls on the name of the Lord will be saved. It might help you to echo this prayer in your heart:

Jesus, like the thief on the cross, I'm not ready to die. I admit that I have gone my own way. I have sinned against you and need your forgiveness. I am sorry for my sins. I want to start over. I want to change.

I know that you are the Son of God. I believe that you died on the cross for my sins and rose again from the dead. Thank you for your great love.

Right now, I open the door. Come in Lord Jesus. Come in as my Savior and forgive me. Come in as my Lord and take over. I want to be saved. I want a relationship with you. Come into my life today and give me a fresh start. Thank you for hearing the cry of my heart. Amen.

Name ________________________________ Date ________________

Individual Response Questions

1. What is the greatest benefit of spiritually starting life over and being *born again?*

2. When is a person ready to become a follower of Jesus?

3. Of the five miracles of salvation, which one is most significant to you? Why?

4. What made Jack Welch believe he could go to heaven? Why do many people agree with him?

5. What was the difference between the two thieves who were crucified with Jesus?

6. What part of this lesson was most meaningful to you?

Personal Assessment

On a scale from 1-6 circle your response (1 means *not true* of you; 6 means *is true* of you).

- My heart is sensitive toward God.

  1 2 3 4 5 6

- I personally claim the five personal miracles connected with salvation.

  1 2 3 4 5 6

- I do not rely on being good enough to "earn" my way to heaven.

  1 2 3 4 5 6

- I have already asked Jesus into my heart.

  1 2 3 4 5 6

- I am ready to open the door and ask Jesus to come into my heart.

  1 2 3 4 5 6

Lesson 5 – God's Beloved Child

§

I'm Wild about You

Nothing compares with being deeply loved. In his book, *The Signature of Jesus,* Brennan Manning tells about a young woman's personal breakthrough during a five-day retreat:

> The small number that attended this retreat allowed for an unusual degree of dialogue and interpersonal communication. One woman in her mid-thirties was conspicuous by her silence. She was so quiet that she neither smiled nor sighed, laughed nor cried, reacted, responded, nor communicated with any of us.
>
> On the afternoon of the fourth day, I invited each person to share what the Lord had been doing in his life the past few days. After a couple of minutes, the uncommunicative woman (whom I shall call Christine) reached for her journal and said, "Something happened to me yesterday, and I wrote it down."
>
> "You were speaking, Brennan, about the compassion of Jesus. You developed the two images of husband (Isaiah 54:5-6) and lover (Hosea 2:16-20). Then you quoted the words of St. Augustine: *Christ is the best husband.*"
>
> "At the end of your talk you prayed that we might experience what you shared. Almost the moment I closed my eyes, I was transported into a large ballroom filled with people."

"I was sitting on a wooden chair when a man approached me, took my hand, and led me onto the floor. He held me in his arms and led me in the dance. The tempo of the music increased and we whirled faster and faster. The man's eyes never left my face. His radiant smile covered me with warmth, delight, and a sense of acceptance. Everyone else on the floor stopped dancing. They were staring at us. The beat of the music increased and we pirouetted around the room in reckless rhythm."

"I glanced at his hands and then I knew. Brilliant wounds of a battle long ago, almost like a signature carved in his flesh. The music tapered to a slow, lilting melody and Jesus rocked me back and forth. As the dance ended, he pulled me close to him. Do you know what he whispered?"

At this moment, every person in the chapel strained forward. Tears rolled down Christine's cheeks. A full minute of silence ensued. Though her face was beaming, the tears kept falling. Finally she spoke. Jesus whispered to me, "Christine, I'm wild about you."

"I stayed in the chapel for over an hour, then went to my room and began to write in my journal what I had just experienced. Suddenly it seemed as if the pen were lifted from my fingers. Again in faith I heard Jesus say, "I'm really wild about you." It was a new experience once more. The love of Jesus swept over me like a gentle tide saturating my being in wonder, bewilderment, peace, certitude and deep worship."

The Bible says we are loved with an everlasting love. Nothing is more personal and powerful than the matchless love that Jesus offers. There is no form of human love that can compare. Most wonderful of all, Jesus knows who we really are and loves who we really are. We can never exaggerate how much Jesus loves us.

The Greatest Relationship

The most wonderful relationship is being God's child. Only God's children recognize that Jesus is truly "wild about them." Only followers of Jesus have this relationship. The Bible says, *Yet to all who receive him, to those who believe in his name, he gave the right to become the children of God* (John 1:12). The Bible teaches that all people are *created by God,* but only those who believe in Jesus are the *children of God.*

Certain spiritual blessings are only granted to the children of God. The children of God are saved, redeemed and forgiven. They are adopted into God's family and added to God's Church. Only the children of God make no apology for believing and following Jesus.

They follow Him as sheep follow a trusted shepherd. Jesus, the Good Shepherd, knows His sheep and they know Him. They recognize His voice and follow His leading. Only the children of God possess the Spirit of God, for it is the Spirit Himself who acknowledges the true children of God. *The Spirit himself testifies with our spirit that we are God's children* (Romans 8:16).

Only God's children are promised life after death. Jesus said, *I am the resurrection and the life. He who believes in me will live even though he dies* (John 11:25). In short, children of God have an identity from their Father in heaven that gives them a sense of security and confidence.

The remaining lessons in this workbook are addressed to *believers* – those who have trusted Jesus as their Savior. If you have yet to trust Jesus for yourself, keep reading. The more you learn about the blessings God gives His children, the more you will desire to know Him personally. Keep asking God to show you the truth about Jesus.

Jesus – God's Beloved Son

While on earth, Jesus described His relationship with God in heaven as one of *Father* and *Son*. This is how Jesus saw Himself and this is how God wants us to see ourselves – as God's beloved children. The first glimpse we get of Jesus' personal relationship with God is at age twelve. He stayed behind in Jerusalem, sitting in the temple courts among the teachers.

When His parents realized that He was not with them, they anxiously looked for Him. Jesus calmly replied, *Why are you searching for me? Didn't you know I had to be in my father's house?* (Luke 2:49). At age twelve, Jesus saw Himself as God's Son and God as His Father.

Another significant episode happened at His baptism when Jesus was around thirty years old. *While He was praying, heaven opened, and the Holy Spirit descended on Him in bodily form like a dove. And a voice came from heaven, 'You are my Son, whom I love; with you I am well pleased'* (Luke 3:21).

Jesus heard His Father's voice publicly affirm His identity. Jesus was God's Son, a beloved and pleasing Son. Wouldn't you agree that Jesus' identity was strengthened after hearing those words? Jesus referred to God as *My Father* over forty times in the gospels:

Matthew 10:32	Whoever acknowledges me before men, I will also acknowledge him before *my Father* in heaven.
Matthew 12:50	Whoever does the will of *my Father* in heaven is my brother and sister and mother.
John 8:19	Then they asked him, "Where is your father?" "You do not know me or *my Father*," Jesus replied. "If you knew me, you would know *my Father* also."
John 14:23	If anyone loves me he will obey my teaching. *My Father* will love him, and we will come to him and make our home with him.
John 16:23	In that day you will no longer ask me anything. I tell you the truth, *my Father* will give you whatever you ask in my name.

Accepted by Jesus

Jesus was secure in His Father's love and confident in His Father's presence. He did not need others to validate His worth. Jesus wants us to be just as secure in God's love as He was. The Father, Son and Holy Spirit accept us as *children of God.*

John 1:12	Yet to all who received him, to those who believed in his name, he gave the right to become *children of God.*
Romans 8:16	The Spirit himself testifies with our spirit that we are *God's children.*
Galatians 3:26	You are all *sons of God* through faith in Jesus Christ.
I John 3:1	How great is the love the Father has lavished on us, that we should be called the *children of God.* And that is what we are.

You may be hesitant to think of God as your *Dad.* Jesus however, taught His followers to use the very personal phrase *Our Father* when they prayed. Likewise, the early believers were encouraged to use the term *Abba,* which, in English, means *Dearest Daddy.*

Matthew 6:9	Pray "*Our Father* in heaven, hallowed be your name..."
Romans 8:15	You did not receive a spirit that makes you a slave again to fear, but you received the Spirit of *sonship*. And by him we cry, *"Abba" Father.*
Galatians 4:6	Because you are sons, God sent the Spirit of his Son into our hearts, the Spirit who calls out, *"Abba Father."* So you are no longer a slave, but a son; and since you are a son, God has made you an heir.

It takes real trust to accept that God is relentlessly tender and compassionate toward us just as we are – not as we should be. God wants us to trust His love. He wants us to stop trying to validate our worth and vindicate our reputation through performance.

An emotionally satisfying relationship with God can never be achieved through rule-keeping or comparing yourself to others. Rather, it begins with our Father in heaven. Through Christ, God gives us our identity – an identity that produces a sense of security and confidence.

When we become obsessed with *pleasing,* we are depending on others to give us an identity. Other people cannot give us our true identity because other people cannot love us like God does. Our identity must come from God alone. **We must learn to see ourselves as accepted by Jesus.**

Access to Jesus

In his book, *Classic Christianity,* Bob George tells the true story about a small boy, not quite three-years old, who grew up in Washington D.C. This three-year-old boy actually lived at the White House.

He would confidently skip past armed servicemen, government officials and staff members. The youngster would run right into the Oval Office and climb onto the lap of the President of the United States. When this happened, influential cabinet members stopped their discussion. Why? The child's name was John-John and his daddy was President John F. Kennedy. When John-John ran into the Oval Office to hug and kiss his daddy, those present simply had to wait.

The years of the Kennedy administration are memorable because there were small children living at the White House. Can you imagine someone objecting? "Now wait just a minute! Don't you know who that man is? He is the President of the United States, the leader of one of the greatest nations on earth. You can't just waltz in here anytime you want; and you can't be sitting on his lap! Who do you think you are?"

John-John would have looked up at his challenger with a grin of total confidence and said, "He's my daddy!" What a difference it makes when a child knows who his father is, and also knows who he is. Our Father in heaven wants us to have the same confidence in approaching Him. It is not a matter of irreverence. Rather, it is grasping what open access to a loving Father means.

Jesus said, *Let the little children come to me, and do not hinder them, for the kingdom of God belongs to such as these* (Luke 18:16). God's children receive strength and hope to face life's tragedies and difficulties.

When my wife, Peggy, was diagnosed with cancer in 1996, she was plagued by many worries. She learned the habit of redirecting her thoughts away from her fears and onto God by repeating the words to the *Cares Chorus*. This song is based on the following instructions: *Cast all your anxiety on God, for he cares for you* (I Peter 5:7). The words to the song are:

> *I cast all my cares upon you. I lay all my burdens down at your feet;*
> *and anytime that I don't know what to do, I will cast all my cares upon you.*

Peggy consciously sang this song day or night, whenever negative thoughts crowded in. As she repeated the words, she pictured herself carrying all of her worries in a big sack and laying them down at the feet of Jesus. Once she had laid her worries down, she envisioned herself crawling up on Jesus' lap. As a child on His lap, she felt secure and safe from all her fears.

Casting your cares upon Jesus gives you peace of mind. God's personal care for you can help you come to terms with the things in life that must be accepted.

Grateful to Jesus

Our disposition reflects the way we see ourselves. Our disposition is our mental frame of mind, emotional tendencies and natural inclinations. This is one clue that helps us discern the difference between a religious person and a true child of God. The prevailing disposition of merely religious people is *entitlement*. The disposition of God's children is *gratitude*.

The Pharisees, who were religious "show-offs," had two telltale flaws: They admired themselves and they despised others. Jewish tax collectors were repulsive because they worked for the Roman government and cheated people. Jesus told this story about a Pharisee and a tax collector:

To some who were confident in their own righteousness and looked down on everybody else, Jesus told this parable: Two men went into the temple to pray, one a Pharisee and the other a tax collector. The Pharisee stood up and prayed about himself: 'God, I thank you that I am not like all other men – robbers, evildoers, adulterers – or even like this tax collector. I fast twice a week and give a tenth of all I get.'

But the tax collector stood at a distance. He would not even look up to heaven, but beat his breast and said, 'God, have mercy on me, a sinner.' I tell you that this man, rather than the other, went home justified before God. For everyone who exalts himself will be humbled, and he who humbles himself will be exalted (Luke 18:9-14).

The Pharisee felt *entitled* and the tax collector felt *unworthy*. If the tax collector received mercy, he considered it a privilege. There are six clear differences between them:

Pharisee	**Tax Collector**
...was blind to his need for God	...was aware of his spiritual condition
...was proud of his own performance	...was conscious of his sin
...felt superior to others	...would not look up to heaven
...told God why he was better than others	...begged God for mercy
...felt entitled to receive approval	...stood at a distance
...believed that acceptance was earned	...knew that acceptance was a gift

Little children do not compare. They receive direct enjoyment from what they have without relating it to something or someone else. In God's kingdom, Jesus sets you free from the prison of jealousy and envy. He enables you to enjoy what you have even if someone else has something larger or better. There is no need for a child of God to compare himself to others.

Living to Please Jesus

Jesus was man as God intended. He did not suffer from a poor self-image. He knew who He was. Our goal is to learn from Jesus. His secret was **humility**. The Bible word for humility is *meekness*. A meek person has a selfless and unassuming nature.

People often associate meekness with weakness. That is not the way it is used in the Bible. Jesus said, *Blessed are those who are humble; who are content with just who they are – no more, no less. The person who is content to be himself is the one who inherits everything from God – everything on earth that cannot be bought* (Matthew 5:5 from The Message).

Jesus invited all people to learn the secret of humility or meekness: *Come to me, all you who are weary and burdened, and I will give you rest. Take my yoke upon you and learn from me, for I am gentle and humble in heart, and you will find rest for your souls. For my yoke is easy and my burden is light* (Matthew 11:28-30).

The burdens Jesus speaks of are not the outward burdens of political oppression, poverty or hard work. He is referring to the inward burden of pride – always pretending and living artificially out of the fear of others' opinions. The *rest* that Jesus offers is simply the release of that burden.

Another burden that many people carry is the burden of not liking themselves. Jesus understands and can offer us release from the inner burden of insecurity and self-hatred. Jesus wants us to see ourselves as persons of value and dignity. God does not impose on us impossible performance standards. God loves us as we are and gives us permission to relax in His love.

The heart's fierce commitment to protect itself from criticism and rejection is a source of inner pain and many sleepless nights. The desire for social approval is universal. Everyone has a circle of people they want to impress. Their approval seems necessary to our happiness.

Jesus' secret was not caring what others think. He knew that the esteem of the world was not worth the effort. The humble person is secure and confident in accepting God's estimate of his life. He knows that the world will never see him as God sees him, and has stopped caring.

Jesus lived His life to please one person – *His Heavenly Father.* His Father was the source of Jesus' identity and the basis of His self-worth. He simply didn't care what others thought as long as God was pleased.

As God's child, the burden of competing with others for recognition, prestige or position is removed. It may take some courage at first, but we are sharing a new and easy yoke with the strong Son of God Himself. Jesus calls it *my yoke*. He walks at one end and we walk at the other.

When we are shaped by Jesus' humility, our need for the approval of others decreases. Our longing for others to validate our worth will never fully be eliminated, but it will diminish. The awareness of being God's beloved child is the key. Our sense of security and confidence comes from our relationship with God.

Where the Angel Kissed Me

In the book, *What Kids Need Most in a Dad,* Tim Hansel tells this tender story:

> There was a teenager who had a very obvious birthmark over much of his face. And yet, it didn't seem to bother him. His self-esteem seemed secure. He related well with the other students and was well liked. He seemed to be in no way self conscious about his very large birthmark, which was obvious to everyone else. Finally, someone asked how this could be.
>
> "Are you aware of the fact that you have this large birthmark on your face?"
>
> "Of course I am," he replied.
>
> "Can you tell me then, why it does not seem to bother you in the slightest?"
>
> The young man smiled and said, "When I was young, my father started telling me that the birthmark was there for two reasons: one, it was where the angel kissed me; two, the angel had done that so that my father could always find me easily in a crowd."
>
> "My Dad told me this so many times with so much love, that as I grew up, I actually began to feel sorry for the other kids who were not kissed by an angel like I was."

Through the gift of His Holy Spirit, God kissed us and left His mark. *Having believed, you were marked with a seal, the promised Holy Spirit* (Ephesians 1:13). He wants us to know that we belong to Him.

Because of Christ's death on the cross, our Father in heaven offers us His acceptance. He looks past the imperfections in our lives and loves us just the way we are. God is your Father. You are His child. One of the greatest blessings God gives us is the privilege of knowing Him as our *Dad*.

Individual Response Questions

1. In your own words, describe the relationship of being God's child.

2. Why is it significant that Jesus referred to God as "my Father?"

3. Like Peggy, what "mental pictures" help you envision having access to Jesus?

4. When are you most inclined to compare yourself with others?

5. When do you worry about what other people think? How does learning humility help?

6. What part of this lesson was most meaningful to you?

Personal Assessment

On a scale from 1-6, circle your response (1 means *not true* of you; 6 means *is true* of you).

- I see God as my heavenly Father; I see myself as His child.

  1 2 3 4 5 6

- When I think of God, I feel a sense of security and confidence.

  1 2 3 4 5 6

- I am not afraid to tell God what is worrying me. I know He understands.

  1 2 3 4 5 6

- I am content with who I am. I rarely compare myself with others.

  1 2 3 4 5 6

- I look at the faults of others with compassion, not a judgmental spirit of superiority.

  1 2 3 4 5 6

Lesson 6 – Let the Past Be Past...At Last

§

I Can't Remember

Brennan Manning, in his book, *The Ragamuffin Gospel*, tells the story of some rumors that were spreading about a Catholic woman. The rumors involved having visions of Jesus.

The reports reached the archbishop. He decided to check her out. The bishop knew that there is a fine line between authentic encounters with God and lunatic people. The bishop asked the woman if it was true that she was having visions of Jesus.

The woman replied, "Yes." He told her that the next time she had a vision, she should ask Jesus to tell her the sins that he confessed in his last confession. The woman was stunned.

"Did I hear you right? You actually want me to ask Jesus to tell me the sins of your past?" The bishop said, "Exactly, please call me if anything happens."

Ten days later the woman notified her spiritual leader of a recent experience. The bishop went to her quickly and looked her straight in the eye. He asked her if she had done what he asked.

"Yes, I asked Jesus to tell me the sins you last confessed." The bishop leaned forward with anticipation. His eyes narrowed. "What did Jesus say?"

She took his hand and gazed deep into his eyes. "His exact words were: *I can't remember.*"

God has totally forgiven us. He is willing to let the past be past. Believing this truth is the only way you will have the ability to forgive others and yourself. Learning to forgive is probably the most difficult lesson for a follower of Jesus to grasp. It begins by first receiving the forgiveness God offers through Jesus.

Luke 24:47	Repentance and *forgiveness of sins* will be preached in His name to all nations...
Acts 2:38	Repent and be baptized, every one of you, in the name of Jesus Christ for the *forgiveness of your sins*.
Acts 10:43	All the prophets testify about Him that everyone who believes in Him receives *forgiveness of sins* through His name.
Acts 13:39	I want you to know that through Jesus the *forgiveness of sins* is proclaimed to you.
Ephesians 1:7	In Him we have redemption through His blood, *the forgiveness of sins*.

Our forgiveness is the result of God's undeserved and unearned love demonstrated by Jesus' death on the cross. Jesus paid a debt He didn't owe to give us a gift we couldn't buy. Forgiveness is a gift to be accepted not a reward to be earned. Since God has forgiven us, He wants us to forgive others.

Matthew 6:12	Forgive us our debts, as we also have *forgiven our debtors*.
Luke 6:37	Do not judge and you will not be judged. Do not condemn and you will not be condemned. *Forgive* and you will be forgiven.
Colossians 3:13	Bear with each other and *forgive whatever grievances* you may have against one another. *Forgive* as the Lord forgave you.

In his wonderful book, *Total Forgiveness*, R.T. Kendall writes,

> When everything in you wants to hold a grudge, point a finger and remember the pain, God wants you to lay it aside. Why? Because when you release it, you will be set free.

Jesus offers all people full and total forgiveness. Although some people do not accept Christ's forgiveness, it is still offered. Jesus died for all people regardless of their response. Every follower of Jesus needs to understand what forgiveness *is not*, what forgiveness *is,* and how to totally forgive others. To provide you a foundation for this important subject, the following is a brief summary adapted from *Total Forgiveness*.

What Total Forgiveness is Not

1. Approval of what they did

   God never approves of our sin. He hates sin. Adam and Eve were banished from the Garden of Eden for their sin. Jesus accepted and forgave sinners, but never condoned their sin.

2. Excusing, justifying, or pardoning what they did

   We do not try to explain away sin or point to extenuating circumstances. Inappropriate behavior is never to be excused. *Justify* means to make right or just. God never calls something that is evil, *right*. Nor does He require us to do so. A pardon is a legal transaction that releases the offender from the consequences of their actions, such as a penalty or sentence. We can forgive and still allow someone to face the consequences of what they did. A repentant criminal may still serve a prison sentence.

3. Reconciliation

   Reconciliation requires participation by *two* people. The other person may not want to see or talk to you. Although it is often desired, forgiveness does not require reconciliation.

4. Denial or Blindness

   Total forgiveness can only be offered after we have admitted what the person actually said or did. Some people willfully pretend or deny that nothing happened. Denial and blindness can be an unconscious or conscious choice to pretend that a sin did not take place. Every sin grieves God and hurts us too. Every sin is important enough to be dealt with on the cross.

5. Forgetting

   We all tend to equate true forgiveness with wiping the memory of the event from our minds. This is not realistic. God doesn't forget our sins – He removes them and chooses to no longer remember them. This is possible because Christ paid our debt. *For I will forgive their wickedness and will remember their sins no more* (Jeremiah 31:34). Through Jesus, our sins are removed. *As far as the east is from the west, so far he has removed our transgressions from us* (Psalm 103:12).

What Total Forgiveness Is

1. Being aware of what someone did and still forgiving him
   Total forgiveness is achieved only when we acknowledge what was done – without any denial or covering up – and still refuse to hold it against the offender.

2. Choosing to not keep score
   Love is a choice to *keep no records of wrongs* (I Corinthians 13:5). Total forgiveness is a choice to *let it go*. People keep score to use it at a later date. Gossiping about the offender is one way of keeping a record of wrongs and punishing him.

   This choice has nothing to do with whether or not the person repented or confessed. Many people we must forgive do not believe they have done anything wrong. Total forgiveness takes place in your heart. *(Of course, incidents of physical or sexual abuse and other illegal behavior must be reported to the appropriate authorities.)*

3. Refusing to get even
   Giving up the natural desire to see someone *get-what-is-coming-to-him* is the essence of total forgiveness. Nothing can ever satisfy a desire to get even. God wants us to forgive and leave justice to the proper authorities.

4. The absence of bitterness
   Bitterness is characterized by strong feelings of hatred and resentment. It heads the list of things that grieve the Holy Spirit. Bitterness builds walls between people. It is very difficult to show kindness while harboring a bitter spirit.

5. Trusting God – not blaming Him
   Although we do not see it at first – and for some it takes a long time – our bitterness is ultimately traceable to God. Our bitterness is often aimed at God because deep in our hearts we believe that He is the one who allowed bad things to happen in our lives.

   God has never sinned and thus He is never guilty. God does not need to be forgiven. God sometimes appears to be unfair, but we must relinquish our bitterness and stop blaming Him before we can move on. We can't draw near to God and blame Him at the same time.

Forgiving Others

The story of Joseph is found in Genesis, chapters 37-50. Joseph was one of twelve brothers. His father, Jacob, treated Joseph with favoritism. He gave him a beautiful robe – a robe he didn't give to his other sons. At age seventeen, God gave Joseph two separate dreams. The dreams revealed that he would someday rule over his family.

Instead of keeping these dreams to himself, he told them to his brothers and father. Jacob's favoritism and Joseph's self-righteousness put a strain on his relationship with his brothers. Out of jealousy and resentment, his brothers sold Joseph as a slave into Egypt (around 1700 BC). To cover up their actions, they told Jacob that wild animals killed Joseph.

In Egypt, the Lord was with Joseph. Potiphar, one of Pharaoh's officials, bought Joseph. Because Potiphar saw that Joseph was successful in everything he did, Potiphar promoted him. He made Joseph head over his household.

Joseph was well built and handsome. One day, Potiphar's wife tried to seduce Joseph. When he refused, she publicly accused Joseph of rape. Potiphar could have executed Joseph but decided to put him in prison.

At this juncture, Joseph had much to be bitter about. There were his brothers who sold him into slavery, Potiphar's wife who lied, and God who let it all happen. In prison, Joseph had two surprising prison mates – Pharaoh's cupbearer and baker. They each told Joseph their dreams. Joseph predicted that the baker would be hanged and the cupbearer would get his job back. Both events took place just as Joseph predicted.

Then, it appears that Joseph began to manipulate his future. He told the cupbearer, *"When all goes well with you, remember me and show me kindness; mention me to Pharaoh and get me out of this prison. For I was forcibly carried off from the land of the Hebrews, and even here I have done nothing to deserve being put in a dungeon"* (Genesis 40:14-15).

Most of us would have done the same thing. But God made Joseph wait in prison two more years. Perhaps Joseph needed to be delivered from bitterness and self-pity. Perhaps Joseph still blamed his brothers, Potiphar's wife and even God for letting it happen. God taught Joseph that He was behind everything that had happened. In prison, Joseph came to terms with God's plan and learned to forgive. Finally, Joseph was ready to move on.

Pharaoh had two troubling dreams that his own magicians couldn't interpret. The situation triggered the cupbearer's memory and he recommended Joseph to Pharaoh. Without Joseph's manipulation, Pharaoh sent for him. God enabled Joseph to interpret Pharaoh's dreams.

Pharaoh was so impressed with Joseph that he made him prime minister of Egypt right on the spot. Through Pharaoh's dreams, God revealed that seven prosperous years would be followed by seven years of worldwide famine.

Due to the famine, his brothers came to Egypt looking for grain. Although they did not recognize him – Joseph recognized them. When the time was right, Joseph revealed himself to his brothers and forgave them from his heart. He held no grudges. He told them that what they intended for evil, God meant for good.

From the life of Joseph, R. T. Kendall teaches us several lessons about total forgiveness:

1. Keep quiet about what they did

   To ensure privacy, Joseph cried out, *"Have everyone leave the room"* (Genesis 45:1). Joseph waited to reveal his identity until there was no one in the room except his brothers. Why? No one in Egypt needed to know what happened. He knew that if the word leaked out that his brothers had sold him into slavery, the Egyptians would hate his brothers.

   For Joseph's brothers, their worst nightmare was that their father would find out about their deception. Joseph instructed his brothers to tell their father one thing: he was alive and well, and had become the prime minister of Egypt. That is all Jacob needed to know. Joseph had no intention of blackmailing his brothers. He was wise and loving.

2. Put them at ease

   Joseph said to his brothers, "I am Joseph. Is my father still living?" But his brothers were not able to answer him, because they were terrified at his presence. (Genesis 45:3). Joseph could have made them acknowledge his power. He could have reminded them of his dreams and their disbelief. But Joseph was not like that.

   He said, *"Come close to me"* (Genesis 45:4). He did not want them to be afraid of him and he longed to embrace every single one of them – which he later did.

3. Help them save face

   Saving face means to preserve one's dignity. To ease their mind, Joseph helped his brothers understand God's plan: *It was to save lives that God sent me ahead of you* (Genesis 45:5). Total forgiveness does not want our offenders to develop chronic guilt feelings.

   People are less upset with themselves for what they did when they are convinced that there is a reason God let it happen. Joseph's kindness toward his brothers did not excuse their behavior, but it did help them see their lives from God's perspective. The perpetual unhappiness that comes from chronic regret does not honor God or help us move forward.

4. Continue to forgive year after year

   All commitments to forgive need renewal. No one said it would be easy. Seventeen years after reuniting with his long-lost son, Jacob died. Joseph's brothers thought Joseph might now take the opportunity to pay them back for all the wrongs they did to him.

   Joseph reassured them by saying, *"Don't be afraid. Am I in the place of God? You intended to harm me, but God intended it for good to accomplish what is now being done, the saving of many lives. So then, don't be afraid. I will provide for you and your children." And he spoke kindly to them* (Genesis 50:19-21).

   The commitment to forgive is a choice that we will have to renew tomorrow, next week, next month and next year. Satan's favorite strategy is to get back into our thought life and tempt us to be bitter. Love pursues a lifestyle of forgiveness.

How Much is Enough?

In his book, *In the Grip of Grace,* Max Lucado tells the story of a 17 year-old boy named Kevin Tunell. On January 1, 1982, Kevin hit and killed 18 year-old Susan Herzog. The case went to Juvenile Court where Kevin was convicted of manslaughter and drunken driving.

After serving his sentence, Kevin spent seven years campaigning against drunken driving – six years more than the court required.

The victim's family sued him for $1.5 million, but settled for $936. This settlement was to be paid back $1.00 each Friday, for 936 weeks – from 1982 to 2000 – eighteen years.

But Kevin kept forgetting to pay the dollar and four times the family took him to court for failure to comply. After one such failure in 1990, Kevin spent another 30 days in jail. Kevin was willing to pay an extra year's worth, if could he have permission to write out one check. The victim's family said, "no." Quoting the mother,

> We want to receive the check every week on time. He must understand that we are going to pursue this until August of the year 2000. We will go back to court every month if we have to.

Max Lucado writes,

> Few would question the anger of the family, but I do have one concern. Are 936 payments enough for the family to demand? When they receive the final payment, will they be at peace? Is eighteen years of restitution sufficient? How much is enough?"

Life is unfair. When we're the victims, how do we get through it? There's more to it than finding a creative way to make the other person pay. In the words of Max Lucado, "Forgiveness is unlocking the door to set someone free and realizing that you were the prisoner."

Tramp for the Lord

Corrie ten Boom was born April 15, 1892 to a watchmaker in Amsterdam, the Netherlands. She followed in her father's footsteps and in 1922 became the first female watchmaker licensed in the Netherlands. In 1923 Corrie helped organize the first girls' club and in the 1930's these clubs grew quite large.

As a follower of Jesus, Corrie was able to rescue many Jews from certain death at the hands of the Nazi SS. Her family took in many children as far back as 1918. In 1940, the Nazis invaded the Netherlands and banned her clubs. By 1942, her family had become very active in the Dutch underground, hiding refugees. Her family's work of saving Jews was motivated by their staunch Christian beliefs.

In 1944, the Nazis arrested the entire ten Boom family. They were first sent to Dutch prisons and finally to the notorious Ravensbruck concentration camp in Germany in September 1944. There, Corrie's sister Betsie died. Corrie was released in December 1944 in what she described later as a clerical error. It so happened that the other women prisoners in the camp were killed the day after her release. In 1946, she went to Germany, and for many years preached in over sixty countries.

During this time she wrote many books including *Tramp for the Lord* and *The Hiding Place*. Her preaching focused on the Christian Gospel, with emphasis on forgiveness. In her book, *Tramp for the Lord,* she tells the story of how, after preaching in Germany in 1947, she was approached by one of the cruelest guards from Ravensbruck camp. She was naturally reluctant to forgive him, but prayed that she would be able to.

Perhaps her most moving testimony was, "For a long time we grasped each other's hands, the former guard and the former prisoner. I had never known God's love as intensely as I did then."

In her post-war experience with victims of Nazi brutality, Corrie observed that those who were able to forgive were best able to rebuild their lives. Having come to terms with the forgiveness Jesus offered her, Corrie learned to forgive and move on.

It's Your Move

Is forgiveness easy? Of course not – but each of us has to decide if it is worth it to go through life holding a grudge and living in a prison of resentment.

When God asks us to forgive, there will not be a dozen choices for us to consider. There will be just one – and an alternative. Remain bitter, or choose to forgive. Your whole future will be conditioned by the choice you make. It's your move. Let the past be past…at last.

Individual Response Questions

1. Why is it so difficult to forgive?

2. Which item in the *forgiveness is not* list is the hardest for you?

3. Which item in the *forgiveness is* list is the hardest for you?

4. How did Joseph illustrate what forgiveness is?

5. Which of the four lessons from the example of Joseph do you need to apply most?

6. What part of this lesson was most meaningful to you?

Personal Assessment

On a scale from 1-6, circle your response (1 means *not true* of you; 6 means *is true* of you).

- Because of God's forgiveness, carrying personal guilt is no longer a problem.

  1 2 3 4 5 6

- I can acknowledge the hurts people have caused me without being bitter.

  1 2 3 4 5 6

- I can forgive and still allow someone to face the consequences of what they did.

  1 2 3 4 5 6

- I forgive when people hurt me.

  1 2 3 4 5 6

- I don't blame God for the things He has allowed in my life that I feel are unfair.

  1 2 3 4 5 6

Lesson 7 – The Forgotten One

§

Life's Greatest Tragedy

Toward the end of A. W. Tozer's life, he had a strange encounter in Toronto, Canada. He describes this unusual experience in his book, *Whatever Happened to Worship?*

> While sitting on a park bench, suddenly a stranger came over and sat down next to me. He smiled at me – a rather puzzled smile I thought.
>
> "Do we know each other?" I asked.
>
> "No, I don't think so. I am in some kind of jam. I think I tripped and fell somewhere in the city and bumped my head. I cannot remember anything for sure. When I woke up I had been robbed. My wallet and all of my papers are gone. I have no identification and I don't know who I am."
>
> "You must have a family somewhere; don't you have any recollection?"
>
> "I probably have, but I cannot recall."
>
> I was about to suggest that the man go to the police for help when a distinguished gentleman looked his way and suddenly began to shout with delight.

He rushed over and called the bewildered man by name. He grabbed him quickly and shook his hand. "Where have you been and what have you been doing? Everyone in the orchestra has been so worried about you."

The lost man was still confused. "Pardon me, sir, but do I know you? I do not recognize you." His friend was shocked.

"What do you mean you don't know me? We came to Toronto together three days ago. We are both members of the Philharmonic Orchestra. You are the first violinist. We've been searching everywhere for you."

The man merely replied, "Hmm...so that's who I am and that's why I am here."

Amnesia is an abnormal condition that is characterized by the loss of memory. Sometimes a person suffering from amnesia cannot remember some of the simplest facts.

One tragedy in the world today is the number of people who suffer from *spiritual amnesia*. They have no idea why they were born. It is not something that many people care to talk about. Their spiritual amnesia has left them hopeless and depressed. The cry of their heart is, "I don't know who I am or why I was born."

God wants to cure our spiritual amnesia. He wants us to recognize Him. One of the consequences of sin is that it has left millions with a *spiritual bump on their head*. Through their disobedience, people are alienated from God and do not know the purpose for their existence.

Because of sin, we have lost our spiritual memory and also our God-given identity. We no longer possess a divine sense of who we are and what we were created to do. In a sense, God is reaching out and asking us, "Don't you know me? Don't you remember who I am and why I made you?" Tragically, many people cannot remember.

The average person in the world today is engaged in a desperate personal search – searching for **the reason they were born.** Though they cannot remember how it happened, they lost God somewhere along the way.

Until our spiritual memory is restored, our life feels aimless and empty. That's why we look for something to give our life meaning. The Holy Spirit can restore our God-given identities. We discover who we are when our spirit is re-united with God's Spirit. Our spiritual amnesia is cured. We know who God is – and who we are.

THE FORGOTTEN ONE

The Scriptures teach that God is both *one* and *three*. God reveals Himself through three Divine Persons. Though God is one, these divine personalities are distinct and unique. Altogether they are called the Godhead or the *Trinity* (three in one).

The first person is God the *Father,* our Creator. The second person is Jesus the *Son,* our Savior. The third person is the *Holy Spirit,* our indwelling personal counselor and guide. They all possess the same divine qualities. All three are eternal with no beginning or end. No one existed before the other. All three are equal. No one is greater or lesser. All three are uncreated, self-existent and infinite. They possess unlimited love, wisdom and power.

Historically, followers of Jesus have always believed in the Trinity, but practically speaking, one member of the Trinity is a forgotten person. **The forgotten one is the Person of the Holy Spirit.**

In much of the world, the Person of the Holy Spirit has been ignored, neglected and forgotten. Dwight L. Moody once said, "True, we have heard of the Holy Spirit, and we have read of Him, but we have little personal knowledge of His attributes, His offices, and His relationship to us."

The views concerning the Holy Spirit held by the average religious person today have almost no practical value. In many Christian circles the Holy Spirit is entirely overlooked. He is nearly non-existent. His presence or absence makes no real difference to anyone.

Few believers see themselves as the channel through whom the Holy Spirit works. Most often, the Holy Spirit is a theory people agree with, but not a reality they experience. A. W. Tozer summarizes the solution to our situation in his book, *The Pursuit of Man:*

> The Holy Spirit does not care whether we write him into our creeds. He is waiting for our emphasis. The followers of Jesus must bring the Spirit of God into the center of their thinking and their lives. The best way to compensate for our neglect of the Holy Spirit is to neglect Him no more.
>
> The Holy Spirit is to be worshiped and obeyed. We should throw open every door and invite Him in. We should surrender to Him every room in the temple of our hearts and insist that he enter our lives and live as if He was Lord and Master within His own dwelling. We should give him the permission to move about freely and change anything He sees so that He is pleased and at home.

Learning about the Holy Spirit and actually knowing Him are two different things. The difference is similar to knowing about food and actually eating it. A person can die of starvation knowing all about bread. Likewise, we can remain spiritually dead while knowing all the facts of Christianity.

Introducing the Person of the Holy Spirit

Jesus lived on earth around thirty-three years. He said, *I came from the Father and entered the world; now I am leaving the world and going back to the Father* (John 16:28). Shortly before He returned to heaven, Jesus promised His disciples that He would send His successor – the Person of the Holy Spirit.

Jesus lives in us through the presence of the Holy Spirit. It may have surprised His disciples when Jesus said, *It is good that I am going away. Unless I go away, the Counselor will not come to you; but if I go, I will send him to you* (John 16:7). John Stott explains:

> The Holy Spirit **universalizes** the presence of Jesus. On earth, the disciples could not enjoy uninterrupted fellowship with their Master, for when they were in Galilee, He might be in Jerusalem. His presence was limited to one place at a time – but no longer. Now, through His Spirit Jesus is with us everywhere.
>
> The Holy Spirit **internalizes** the presence of Jesus. He said to his disciples, *You know him (the Spirit of Truth, the Counselor), for he lives with you and will be in you. I will not leave you as orphans; I will come to you* (John 14:17-18). On earth, Jesus was with them and could teach them, but he could not enter their personality and change them from within. Now, through the Holy Spirit, Christ dwells in our hearts and does His transforming work there.

If you are a follower of Jesus, the Holy Spirit lives in you. Nothing could be more beneficial to your spiritual development than to deepen your personal acquaintance with Him.

Who He Is

The Holy Spirit is God. He is just as eternal as God the Father and Jesus the Son. Every quality belonging to Almighty God is freely attributed to the Holy Spirit. He is indivisible from the Father and the Son. The Holy Spirit is one with God just as your spirit is one with you.

The Holy Spirit is spirit not matter. He has no color, size, weight, or material substance. He exists invisibly. He is unseen, but He exists just as surely as you do. Just because He is unseen does not mean He is not real.

The Holy Spirit is a Person. The Holy Spirit is a spiritual being. He is a living personality. While He is not a human, He possesses every quality that we associate with any personality, such as intelligence, emotion and will. He communicates with us through the familiar avenue of our personality. He can feel sympathy, affection and compassion. He thinks, sees, hears, speaks, enjoys, desires and suffers as any other person may.

When God's Word says, *And do not grieve the Holy Spirit of God* (Ephesians 4:30), it is telling us that He loves us so much that when we insult, ignore, resist or doubt Him, He is grieved. Like any person, a relationship with Him can be cultivated.

Knowing someone well requires more than one conversation. Likewise, through frequent communication, we come to know Him better. Dr. R. A. Torrey once said,

> I know of no thought that is more calculated to keep us humble than the great biblical truth of the Holy Spirit as a divine person coming to take up His dwelling in our hearts. He takes possession of our lives and uses us as He, in His infinite wisdom, sees fit.

The Holy Spirit is the personal successor of Jesus Christ. In the individual life of every believer, He is God living with us and in us. He is Almighty God in contact with humans. He does for people what Jesus did for people – He opens hearts and changes lives. He teaches and guides. He is as real and actual to us as was the presence of Jesus with His own disciples.

The Holy Spirit is not merely a force. It is unwise and unbiblical to think of the Holy Spirit as an influence, a stimulus, a sensation, or a set of ideas. We are filled with a Person – the indwelling life of Christ Himself. He is a Person with power, not an impersonal force that manipulates and sways people. The Holy Spirit is not something a crowd of people can generate.

We must resist thinking of Him as a *jolt of energy* or an emotional experience. To think of Him in these ways is to make Him non-personal and non-individual. He is a Person, a real spiritual being whom we can know.

His Role

The Holy Spirit's goal is to **penetrate and teach**. He penetrates our hearts to be our primary Teacher. *The Holy Spirit, whom the Father will send in my name, will teach you all things and will remind you of everything I have said to you* (John 14:26). The role of *Indwelling Teacher* is what distinguishes the Holy Spirit's ministry from Jesus' ministry with His apostles.

Jesus taught His followers externally. The Holy Spirit teaches us internally. He can penetrate our mind, emotions and will from within. He can completely penetrate our human spirit and make room for Himself without expelling or impairing anything essential to our own personality.

Without question, one of the most remarkable Bible promises is that Jesus Christ Himself through the Holy Spirit will actually enter a heart, settle down and be at home there. The Holy Spirit will live in any human heart that welcomes Him. In his book, *The Pursuit of Man,* A. W. Tozer writes,

> How can one personality penetrate another? The candid answer is that we do not know. But a near understanding may be made by borrowing a simple analogy from the old devotional writers of several hundred years ago.
>
> Imagine placing a piece of iron in a fire and blowing up the coals. At first you have two distinct substances – iron and fire. When you insert the iron in the fire you achieve the penetration of the iron and you not only have the iron in the fire but the fire in the iron as well. Two distinct substances have co-mingled and penetrated one another to a point where the two have become one.
>
> In a similar manner the Holy Spirit penetrates our human spirit. In the whole experience we remain our very selves. There is no destruction of substance. Each remains a separate being as before; the difference is that now the Spirit penetrates and fills our personality and we are experientially one with God.

This initial invasion of our lives begins to cure our spiritual amnesia. We recognize who we really are. *The Spirit himself testifies with our spirit that we are God's children* (Romans 8:16). Authentic disciples know their heavenly Father.

Paul told the Corinthians, *He anointed us, set his seal of ownership on us, and put His Spirit in our hearts as a deposit guaranteeing what is to come* (II Corinthians 1:22). A seal is a mark of ownership. The Holy Spirit is God's seal, branding us as belonging to Him forever. Conversely, *If anyone does not have the Spirit of Christ, he does not belong to Christ* (Romans 8:9).

Another role of the Holy Spirit is to assure us that we are never alone. Since He is with us, God is with us. He walks with us every day of our lives. If we were suddenly transferred to heaven itself, we wouldn't be any closer to God than we are now, for God, by His Spirit is already here.

When Dwight Moody was asked how he remained so intimate in his relationship with Christ he replied, "There isn't any problem in my life, there isn't any uncertainty in my work, but I turn and speak to Him as naturally as to someone in the same room, and I have done it these years because I can trust Jesus."

One reason the Holy Spirit is given to us is to prove that God has the power to change human nature. The proof the world wants lies in the invisible, unseen power of the Holy Spirit transforming the human heart into the likeness of Jesus. The Holy Spirit's role is to make sure the gospel message is visibly seen, not just heard.

His Attributes

If you wonder what the Holy Spirit is like, all you have to do is look at Jesus. The Holy Spirit is exactly like Jesus. Whatever you find Jesus saying, feeling, and doing, you will also find the Holy Spirit saying, feeling and doing.

Jesus is the epitome of love, kindness, gentleness and patience. He is completely approachable and puts people at ease. That is exactly what the Holy Spirit is like. Just as no one had to fear Jesus, no one ever needs to be afraid of the Holy Spirit. Like Jesus, the Holy Spirit can be identified by His truth, love and power.

He is truth. The Holy Spirit confirms Jesus as the Son of God. When Jesus was baptized, the seal of approval on his life was the presence of the Holy Spirit. *And as He was praying, heaven was opened and the Holy Spirit descended on Him in bodily form like a dove. And a voice came from heaven: "You are my Son, whom I love; with you I am well pleased"* (Luke 3:21-22).

The Holy Spirit convicts hearts. *When he comes, he will convict the world of guilt in regard to sin, and righteousness and judgment* (John 16:8). Only the Holy Spirit has the power to convict people of their need for God. The Holy Spirit shows us our sin and creates within us a desire to get right with God.

The Holy Spirit uses Scriptural truths to pierce our hearts and wake us up. When a person hears the living God speaking to his conscience, it is the voice of the Holy Spirit speaking.

He is love. Jesus promised that the Holy Spirit would be a loving friend – a personal guide who would be with you and live in you forever. Jesus said, *I will not leave you as orphans, I will come to you. We will come to him and make our home with him* (John 14:18, 23).

In his book, *The Christ of the Forty Days*, A. B. Simpson tells the story about a mother who sent her son to an English boarding school that was very far from her home.

She was very troubled to learn that the school had a rule that only permitted her to visit her son once every two weeks. This was more than her heart could stand and so, all unknown to her boy or his teachers, she rented a little attic apartment overlooking the school.

While her son never knew, she would sit in the upper room with her eyes on her little boy as he played in the schoolyard or studied in the classroom. He could not see her nor did he even dream she was there. But if he got hurt, cried, called her name or needed her for a moment, she was within his reach.

Just like the loving mother, the Holy Spirit has His eye upon His beloved children night and day. Although we do not physically see His face, He is there every day. We can believe His promise and assume the reality of His presence. Because He is so close by, we are never alone and never defenseless. Nothing can separate us from His love.

He is power. The Bible uses many powerful images to describe the Person of the Holy Spirit. He is described as a mighty and mysterious wind (John 3 & Acts 2), living and flowing water (John 4 & 7) and a purifying, consuming fire (Matthew 3 & Acts 2).

But the Holy Spirit is more than a mere force of nature like wind, water or fire. He is a divine Person who possesses divine power. It is vital to learn that the Holy Spirit is a Person, not a force.

If you think of Him as a force, you will be tempted to try to get hold of the Holy Spirit's power to use it to accomplish your agenda. But if you think of the Holy Spirit as a Person, you will want Him to get hold of you, and use you according to His will.

His Personality

Every person has a personality. The three most obvious personality traits of the Holy Spirit are His individuality, His activity and His leadership:

His Individuality

The Holy Spirit has an intelligent mind, genuine feelings and a decisive will:

He Knows	The Holy Spirit knows the thoughts of God.	I Corinthians 2:11
He Feels	Do not grieve the Holy Spirit of God.	Ephesians 4:30
He Decides	He gives gifts to each man, just as He determines.	I Corinthians 12:11

His Activity

The actions of the Holy Spirit are those only a person could perform:

He Searches	The Spirit searches and reveals the deep things of God.	I Corinthians 2:10
He Prays	The Spirit Himself intercedes for you.	Romans 8:26
He Teaches	The Holy Spirit will teach you all things.	John 14:26
He Speaks	The Holy Spirit said, 'Set apart Barnabas and Saul…'	Acts 13:2
He Leads	All who are being led by the Spirit are sons of God.	Romans 8:14
He Alters	The Spirit transforms from one degree to another.	II Corinthians 3:18
He Works	He is able to do more than all we ask or imagine.	Ephesians 3:20

His Leadership

The Holy Spirit is Jesus' successor and is qualified to lead God's people:

He's Real	You know him for he lives with you and will be in you.	John 14:17
He's Divine	I will send you a Counselor who is from the Father.	John 15:26
He's Vital	Stay until you have been clothed with power from on high.	Luke 24:49
He's Loving	We will make our home with you.	John 14:18, 23
He's Wise	The Spirit of truth will guide you into all truth.	John 16:13
He's Strong	The one in you is greater than the one in the world.	I John 4:4
He's Loyal	He will be with you forever.	John 14:16

If we ignore the personal counselor God has sent into our hearts, we will naturally turn to human resources. The Spirit's wisdom will be replaced by human psychology. The Spirit's love will be replaced by human methods. The Spirit's power will be replaced by human effort.

Available to God

The mother of Jesus was a woman named Mary. God sent the angel Gabriel to inform Mary that God chose her for a special purpose. *You will be with child and give birth to a son, and you are to give him the name Jesus* (Luke 1:31). Naturally, Mary was surprised and wondered how this could happen since she was a virgin.

The angel answered, *"The Holy Spirit will come upon you, and the power of the Most High will over-shadow you. So the holy one to be born will be called the Son of God." "I am the Lord's servant," Mary answered. "May it be to me as you have said"* (Luke 1:35, 38).

When Mary tried to explain that she was a virgin, God helped her understand her role. In effect, God said, "Mary, I am not asking you to make this happen. My Holy Spirit will provide the power for this miraculous pregnancy." In other words, "I'll do everything. I just need your body. Can I count on you? Will you trust me?"

This encounter between Mary and the angel helps us understand what God wants from people. God is looking for our availability. God wanted Mary to offer Him her body. **Living for Jesus is voluntarily consenting to let God use your life.**

E. M. Bounds writes, "Nothing is too hard for God to do if He can only find the right kind of person to do it." Today, God is looking to indwell your body. God has a plan in mind just for you. Like Mary, God wants you to be available to the Holy Spirit. Will you invite Him in and be conscious of His presence?

Whose Picture Do You See?

A follower of Jesus is the temple of the Holy Spirit. Jesus lives in us through the Person of the Holy Spirit. This is certainly an overwhelming concept. In his book, *Wholly Sanctified,* A. B. Simpson uses a simple illustration of a leather purse, a silver case, and a golden locket to explain this important reality. Use your respectful imagination and picture Simpson explaining this illustration:

> "Ladies and gentlemen, I have in my hand a small, common leather purse." The people watching noticed that it was tough and worn. It had been touched and handled many times.

> "Let this common leather purse represent your human body. This is the outward part of you – the visible and physical part. But there's more to you than just your body. Let's look inside."
>
> Inside the purse was a shiny silver case. "This silver case represents your human soul. This is the inward part of you. The silver case is your personality; your mind, emotions and will. But there's still more to you. Let's look further inside."
>
> Simpson touched a small spring and the silver case opened. Inside the silver case was a beautiful golden locket. "This golden locket is your human spirit. It is the deepest part of you that was created for God Himself. This is His throne, a shrine reserved for Himself and no one else."
>
> The crowd listened carefully to every word. Now was the moment of truth for everyone present. "Within the golden locket is a devoted place, set with beautiful and precious gems. It is a place reserved for a single picture."
>
> "Let's open the locket and ask a personal and penetrating question. When you open your locket what do you see? Do you see a picture of Jesus? Or is your locket empty?"
>
> "If you see the face of Jesus, you know you are His temple. You belong to Him and He belongs to you. If your locket is empty, you know that Jesus is still waiting to enter your heart."

God doesn't live in buildings. He lives in those who follow Jesus. *God's house* is not a church building – it's the human heart. It doesn't matter who you are. If you open the *golden locket* of your heart and see nothing, you are not yet His temple. But if you see the face of Jesus, you know that He lives within you. You are His temple – His dwelling place on earth. Will you invite Him in? Will you be conscious of His presence? He wants you to recognize His role in your life.

Individual Response Questions

1. What new perspectives did you discover about the Holy Spirit?

2. What is the difference between *knowing about* the Holy Spirit and *knowing* the Holy Spirit?

3. Which of the three personality traits of the Holy Spirit are most familiar to you?

4. How does the Holy Spirit counsel and guide you?

5. How does viewing your body as God's temple change your words and actions?

6. What part of this lesson was most meaningful to you?

Personal Assessment

On a scale from 1-6, circle your response (1 means *not true* of you; 6 means *is true* of you).

- My God-given identity gives me security and confidence.

  1 2 3 4 5 6

- I make getting to know the Holy Spirit a priority.

  1 2 3 4 5 6

- I am consciously opening more of my life to the influence of the Holy Spirit.

  1 2 3 4 5 6

- When I grieve the Holy Spirit, I am quickly aware of it.

  1 2 3 4 5 6

- I am constantly aware of the Holy Spirit's presence.

  1 2 3 4 5 6

Lesson 8 – The Struggle Within

§

Spiritual Stagnation

Ron Bennett, in his book *Intentional Disciplemaking,* recalls the events that surrounded the birth of their first-born son, Bryan. When Bryan was born in May 1975, Ron and his wife Mary thought everything was fine.

But one hour after his birth the doctor feared brain damage. Ron and Mary hastily signed the necessary forms and the hospital staff transported Bryan to a neo-natal intensive care unit sixty miles away. Ron writes,

> Bryan is now twenty-five years old, but he has never walked, never seen the sun and never said, 'Mom' or 'Dad'. He has never played baseball, run through a sprinkler or given us a hug.
>
> Immediately after his birth, Bryan became a prisoner in his own body when severe brain damage created multiple handicaps that permanently stifled his maturation process. Consequently, he has had twenty-five years of living, but only nine months of normal, healthy development.
>
> As his parents we love him deeply – as much as we love our other three children. Yet his inability to mature has robbed him and us, of God's design for life.

> We have learned to accept Bryan just as he is – to relate to him at his level of understanding. Because he can't see, we simply touch. Because he can't speak, we talk. Because he can't reach out to us, we hug him.
>
> Still, we occasionally wonder what life would be like had Bryan grown up. God must feel a similar sadness and pain when his children get "stuck" at spiritual infancy, childhood or adolescence – when they never reach spiritual adulthood with all the privileges and responsibilities it entails.
>
> Of course God's love remains constant and immeasurable regardless. But like a human parent, God can also feel disappointment, pain and loss.

Becoming like Jesus is not automatic. It requires our cooperation and obedience. God wants us to avoid *prolonged spiritual infancy* – an abnormal spiritual condition that causes a person to stagnate; to never mature beyond the level of a spiritual infant.

The key to letting God re-train your heart is openness and receptivity. At first this may sound simple, but it's not. Every follower of Jesus discovers within himself a spirit of resistance toward God's heart-shaping activity. What is the source of this struggle? Jesus calls it the *self-life*.

The Flesh and the Self-Life

The Bible uses two terms to describe the fallen nature of man: *flesh* and *self*. These terms refer to the dark side of the human heart that does not naturally cooperate with God. When the Scriptures refer to *the flesh* it does not mean your skin. Our *flesh* refers to our old disposition (also called the old self) – the way we lived before Jesus came into our hearts.

The *flesh* is the natural way a person lives without God. These natural tendencies are personal strategies we have developed to relieve the pain of living in a fallen world. The *flesh* has a natural resistance to God and His ways. Every natural thought, feeling or behavior that is not derived from the Spirit of God is the *flesh*. What our *flesh* wants us to do is the opposite of what *God* wants us to do. This is an inward spiritual battle with which we are all familiar. The apostle Paul clearly describes it this way:

> *Live by the Spirit and you will not gratify the desires of the flesh. The flesh desires what is contrary to the Spirit and the Spirit what is contrary to the flesh.*
>
> *They are in conflict with each other, so that you do not do what you want. The acts of the flesh are obvious: sexual immorality, impurity, debauchery, idolatry and witchcraft; hatred, discord, jealousy, fits of rage, selfish ambition, dissension, factions, and envy; drunkenness, orgies and the like.*
>
> *I warn you as I did before, that those who live like this will not inherit the kingdom of God* (Galatians 5:16-21).

The *flesh* is what comes naturally. Our *flesh* is all of our natural instincts and common sense apart from God. It always possesses an independent approach to life. When we forget or ignore God's ways, this natural approach always makes more sense.

Jesus taught that to make progress in following Him, every believer must come to terms with his *life* and his *self* – in short, his *self-life*. The *self-life* within every believer is strong. It has the power to resist Jesus and in turn, pursue what can be gained from the world. What our *self-life* wants us to do is totally different than what *God* wants us to do. In Luke 9:23-25, Jesus said,

> *If any man would come after me, he must deny himself and take up his cross daily and follow me. For whoever wants to save his life will lose it, but whoever will lose his life for me will save it. What good is it for a man to gain the whole world, and yet lose or forfeit his very self?*

Something We Are

These are not pleasant things to discuss, but God wants us to recognize the real, yet subtle power of the *self-life*. It covers over our hearts like a clear, invisible lens. The human eye is scarcely conscious of its own existence. It sees everything in front of it, yet never sees itself.

In the same way, we don't see the *self-life* itself, but we always see the world through it. The lens of the *self-life* affects our perception of everything and everyone. It is composed of self-sins. To be more specific, self-sins are: self-righteousness, self-pity, self-confidence, self-sufficiency, self-admiration, self-love and others like these.

These are not something **we do**, but something **we are**. That's why we don't readily acknowledge them. They dwell too deeply within us to be easily recognized. We can usually spot them in others, but rarely in ourselves. Most followers of Jesus are blind to their own *self-life* until the light of God's Spirit exposes it.

The *self-life* is demanding and divided. Selfish people are demanding. They are self-seeking and self-centered. Our natural inbred tendency to demand our rights and insist on our own way is what Jesus deals with as He works on our hearts. In addition, our *self-life* desires many things. Apart from God, our thoughts and feelings are fragmented. We want to do what is good, but also want to get our own way. Our will is splintered. Satan often uses our divided heart to defeat us. Jesus wants to transform our character so that it is single-minded, like His.

Our earthly struggle with our *self-life* will never completely be eliminated. Jesus said that denying *self* and taking up our cross is a daily decision. Furthermore, the power of our *self-life* cannot be diminished by mere study, instruction and information. God's heart-shaping work is experiential, not academic. Can taking a class cure cancer?

God miraculously reduces the power of the *self-life* when we surrender our will and put everything into the Lord's hands. This is the effect of taking up our cross. It brings us to the end of ourselves. The pain of the cross is real. It hurts to learn humility. It hurts when our dreams die. It hurts when we lose our rights. It hurts to admit that we don't have the strength to make our lives come out the way we want. In his book, *Christ in You,* A. B. Simpson writes,

> It is said that Alexander the Great had a famous horse that nobody could ride. Alexander spent much time trying to break it. In the course of his efforts, he saw that the horse was afraid of his own shadow. Leaping into the saddle one day and turning the horse's head to the sun, he struck his spurs into the flanks of the noble steed and dashed off like lightning. From that moment on, the fiery charger was thoroughly subdued and it never gave its master any trouble again. It could no longer see its own shadow.

The way to deal with the *self-life* is to focus on Jesus. In doing so, we will no longer see the shadow of *self.* By fixing our gaze on Jesus, we grant the Holy Spirit access to our mind, emotions and will. Though our *self-life* will never be eliminated, it doesn't have to control us.

When Jesus is allowed to form our thoughts, shape our desires and direct our will, He gains full possession of us and governs our actions. The result is people see Jesus in us. Let's identify the choices that give the Holy Spirit greater access and help us become more like Christ.

The Heart God Wants

The call to be Christ's disciple is personal and practical. God doesn't want to educate us. He wants to transform us. He wants His disciples to experience on-going transformation into the image of Jesus. Experiencing Christ-likeness does not happen by focusing on what you don't want to be. We cannot become like Jesus by constantly criticizing our own behavior.

We become like Jesus by looking at Jesus. As we fix our eyes on Jesus, our disposition begins to look like His. God's Spirit will change us when we cultivate a *seeking heart*, a *separated heart,* and a *surrendered heart*. Your choice to pursue such a heart is not a requirement for your salvation, but it is a condition for becoming like Jesus.

Seeking Heart

Jesus had a seeking heart. He said, *I seek not to please myself but him who sent me* (John 5:30). The Bible says, *Without faith it is impossible to please God, because anyone who comes to him must believe that he exists and that he rewards those who earnestly seek him* (Hebrews 11:6). **God is pleased with a seeking heart**.

David was the second king of Israel. God chose him because the greatest passion of his life was to seek after God. *Look to the LORD and his strength; seek his face always* (I Chronicles 16:11).

David charged his son Solomon, *Now devote your heart and soul to seeking the LORD your God* (I Chronicles 22:19). In every situation, David looked to God. *I sought the LORD, and he answered me; he delivered me from all my fears* (Psalm 34:4). **God loves a seeking heart.**

Simeon was a very old man who lived in Jerusalem. He was a good and righteous man who wanted, more than anything else, to see the Messiah before he died. Shortly after Jesus' birth, the Holy Spirit led Simeon into the temple.

There he encountered Joseph and Mary (the earthly parents of Jesus). Simeon was privileged to take baby Jesus into his arms and hold Him. Simeon blessed God for allowing him to see the One who would bring salvation to all nations (Luke 2:25-35). **God directs a seeking heart.**

Jesus stressed the importance of trusting God by not worrying about physical needs. *Seek first his kingdom and his righteousness, and all these things will be given to you as well* (Matthew 6:33). **God takes care of the seeking heart.**

Our Father in heaven gladly hears our prayers. *Ask and it shall be given to you; seek and you will find; knock and the door will be opened to you* (Matthew 7:7). **God answers a seeking heart.**

Nothing shows Jesus that we are more open and receptive to His will than a seeking heart. He honors our desire to know Him. In his book, *That Incredible Christian,* A. W. Tozer writes, *Every man is as close to God as he wants to be*. The key is the desire of your heart.

God can distinguish between wanting and wishing. *Wanting* represents a whole-hearted desire. When we really want something we seek after it. *Wishing* is passive and non-committal. Many people may wish they were different than they are, but they have no intention to change.

In financial planning discussions I often ask my clients, *What's more important in life than money?* Their answers reveal what their hearts really value. Whatever we value, we seek. God wants a seeking heart. This is the foundation for being changed into the likeness of Jesus.

Separated Heart

Paul prayed, *May God himself sanctify you through and through. May your whole spirit, soul and body be kept blameless at the coming of our Lord Jesus Christ* (I Thessalonians 5:25). To sanctify means to *separate* for a special purpose. God wants His followers to be separated from the world and set apart for Him.

Separating from the world does not mean refusing to have contact with people who do not obey God. Jesus associated with all types of people, yet He separated Himself to God. Separating yourself to God means removing whatever may be hindering your relationship with Jesus. This is not easy because it often involves making a conscious choice to let go of things or relationships that we have cherished for years.

King Solomon was the son of David and the third king of Israel. In his day, Solomon was called the wisest man in the world. The Bible says, *The whole world sought audience with Solomon to hear the wisdom God had put in his heart* (I Kings 10:27).

Before David died, he instructed Solomon to do what God told him: *walk in the commandments in the Law of Moses*. If he did, God would bless him. One of those commandments involved not marrying women from nations that did not follow the Lord. This command reminded everyone that God's people are to be a separated people. Notice what happened:

> *King Solomon however loved many foreign women. They were from the nations about which the LORD had told the Israelites, 'You must not intermarry with them, because they will surely turn your hearts after their gods.'*
>
> *Nevertheless, Solomon held fast to them in love. He had seven hundred wives of royal birth and three hundred concubines, and his wives led him astray.*
>
> *As Solomon grew old, his wives turned his heart after other gods, and his heart was not fully devoted to the LORD his God, as the heart of David his father had been* (I Kings 11:1-4).

In contrast to Solomon was Daniel. After years of disobedience, God allowed the king of Babylon to destroy Jerusalem and take many Jewish people into captivity (605 BC). Among those taken was a young man named Daniel.

The king noticed that Daniel was handsome and intelligent. He was allowed to enter a three-year training program with other young leaders. This program involved learning the language, literature, and customs of the Babylonians.

One of the benefits of the program was getting to eat the food and wine from the king's table. *But Daniel resolved not to defile himself with the royal food and wine, and he asked the chief official for permission not to defile himself in this way* (Daniel 1:8).

Daniel asked for only vegetables and water. At first, the official was afraid, but then gave permission for a ten-day trial. At the end of the trial period, Daniel and his friends looked healthier and better nourished than any of the young men who ate the royal food. God honored Daniel's commitment to live a separated life.

> *At the end of the time set by the king to bring them in, the chief official presented them to Nebuchadnezzar. The king talked with them, and he found none equal to Daniel, Hananiah, Mishael and Azariah; so they entered the king's service.*
>
> *In every manner of wisdom and understanding about which the king questioned them, he found them ten times better than all the magicians and enchanters in his whole kingdom* (Daniel 1:18).

When our older daughter, Carey, entered the first grade, Peggy was concerned about the words she would hear on the playground. Peggy told Carey, "Honey, if you hear any words at school that you have never heard before, I want you to tell me the words before you repeat them." Carey responded, "Mom, if this is really that important, can't you just make me a list of these words?"

Throughout the Bible, there are many lists that define behavior God approves or disapproves. These lists are as different as light and darkness. *You were once darkness, but now you are light in the Lord. Live as children of light* (Ephesians 5:8). Having a separated heart means recognizing that light and darkness cannot co-exist.

Our new birth results in new behavior. *Sin* and the child of God are incompatible. They may occasionally meet, but they cannot live in harmony. God's people must not live like the world. *Anyone who chooses to be a friend of the world becomes an enemy of God* (James 4:4).

One of Satan's master strategies to defile a follower of Jesus is to convince him that light and darkness can **co-exist** peacefully. Solomon thought that his foreign wives would not hurt him. By contrast, Daniel kept his distance from the Babylonian lifestyle.

Many followers of Jesus know that nothing drains their spiritual strength like flirting with compromising situations. Satan wants to draw us into unholy alliances, partnerships, and relationships. Satan wants us to partner with ungodly people who will deplete our spiritual strength. Satan wants us to forget that light and darkness cannot co-exist.

It is often necessary to set family boundaries that reinforce moral standards. When our daughters were growing up in our home, Peggy and I established a family rule that we would only view movies with a G or PG rating. This rule was for every member of the family (including us). Once, this included taking our twelve-year-old daughter out of school for one day while her class viewed a PG-13 movie.

When our daughters were invited to parties or sleepovers, we telephoned the parents in advance to inform them of our family policy. When Carey and Crystal were older, they informed their friends of the "family rule." The school, other parents and their friends respected our stand.

I was once required to attend a company meeting in Iowa. Several co-workers invited me to ride with them. They revealed their intention to pick up a case of beer after the meeting and drink during the ride home.

I was uncomfortable with the situation, including the illegality of an open container. I informed them that if this was the plan, I would find another way to the meeting. Even though they decided not to purchase any alcohol, some were very upset with me. It was difficult because these people are my friends. I did not want to isolate myself, but in this situation I needed to separate.

Jesus is God's light to the world. He did not isolate Himself from sinful people, but did not participate in sinful behavior. **God honors a separated heart.**

Surrendered Heart

Jesus had a surrendered heart. To reflect the likeness of Jesus, we must do more than merely separate ourselves from the wrong influences. To surrender means to yield your will to Jesus. Jesus wants us to say ***no to sin*** and ***yes to Him.*** He wants us to voluntarily offer Him our lives, our relationships and our future. Jesus wants us to abandon the outcome to God.

In general, the Scriptures reveal that the Lord does not fully bless a man until He has first conquered him. This is not a popular idea in an age that promotes self-sufficiency. To be conquered by God is to win blessings found nowhere else.

One of the most dramatic pictures of a surrendered heart is found in the story of Abraham and his son, Isaac. When God called Abraham, he was seventy-five years old. Though childless, God promised Abraham and Sarah that He would miraculously provide them with a son.

Twenty-five years later, God fulfilled His promise. When Isaac was born, Abraham was one hundred and Sarah was ninety-nine years old. In his book, *The Pursuit of God,* A. W. Tozer offers this opinion to help us understand what happened between Abraham and God after the birth of Isaac. He writes,

> Abraham was old when Isaac was born, old enough to be his grandfather, and the child became at once the delight and idol of his heart. From the moment he stooped to take the tiny form awkwardly in his arms, he was an eager love slave to his son.
>
> God went out of his way to comment on the strength of this affection. And it is not hard to understand. The baby represented everything sacred to his father's heart: the promises of God, the covenants, the hopes of the years, and the long messianic dream.

> As he watched him grow from babyhood to manhood, the heart of the old man was knit closer with the life of his son, till at last the relationship bordered on the perilous. It was then that God stepped in to save both father and son from the consequences of an un-cleansed love.
>
> *Take your son, your only son Isaac, whom you love and go to the region of Moriah. Sacrifice him there as a burnt offering on one of the mountains I will tell you about* (Genesis 22:2).
>
> The sacred writer spares us a close-up of the agony that night when the aged man had it out with God. God let the suffering old man go through with it up to the point where He knew that there would be no retreat, and then forbid him to lay a hand upon the boy.
>
> To the wondering patriarch He now says in effect, *"It's all right Abraham. I never intended that you should actually slay the lad. I only wanted to remove him from the temple of your heart that I might reign unchallenged there. Take the lad back to your tent."* Now he was a man wholly surrendered, utterly obedient – a man who possessed nothing.

This was a hard lesson from God, but it was effective. Abraham now possessed nothing on earth that he could not part with. On the night before His crucifixion, Jesus faced a similar situation.

For Jesus, it was a choice of offering up His own life. As he prayed in the Garden of Gethsemane, His prayer reveals that He had a choice to make: *Father, if you are willing, take this cup from me; yet not my will, but yours be done* (Luke 22:42). Jesus yielded His will and was obedient unto death. With His eyes fixed on pleasing His Father, He endured the cross. Jesus abandoned the outcome to God.

Both Jesus and Abraham learned a spiritual secret that cannot be learned in a theological school. It is the secret of surrender. This lesson can only be learned in the school of renunciation.

There are no books on systematic theology that can teach *surrender.* These truths cannot be learned by rote as one would learn the facts of physical science. The blessed and bitter lessons of the surrendered heart are only learned by personal experience. Every follower of Jesus must brace himself when God leads him down the path of surrender. Will you let him direct your will? **God blesses and uses a surrendered heart.**

Individual Response Questions

1. In your own words, describe the *self-life*. How have you experienced its influence?

2. How does your *self-life* and the *flesh* slow your spiritual growth?

3. Which heart do you need to cultivate: Seeking? Separated? Surrendered?

4. Did this lesson discourage you? Why?

5. Did this lesson encourage you? Why?

6. What part of this lesson was most meaningful to you?

Personal Assessment

On a scale from 1-6, circle your response (1 means *not true* of you; 6 means *is true* of you).

- I can easily name the areas where my natural instincts fight against God.

  1 2 3 4 5 6

- I have strong spiritual desires. I am constantly seeking to know God better.

  1 2 3 4 5 6

- I consciously separate myself from sinful influences.

  1 2 3 4 5 6

- My life demonstrates that doing *God's will* is more important than doing *my will*.

  1 2 3 4 5 6

- I willingly yield to God and trust the outcome to Him.

  1 2 3 4 5 6

Lesson 9 – Extreme Makeover

§

Spiritual Expectations

Hank is a man John Ortberg describes in his book, *The Life You've Always Wanted*. Do you know anyone who fits this description?

Hank believed in Jesus since he was a boy. He was now in his 60's. By name, people knew who Hank was, but no one really knew Hank, *the person*. Hank had difficulty loving his wife. His children could not speak freely with him and felt no affection from him. He was not concerned for the poor and less fortunate.

He had little tolerance for those who didn't go to church. He tended to judge people harshly. One day, a leader in the church asked him, "Hank, are you happy?" Without smiling, he responded, "Yes." "Well then," replied the church leader, "tell your face."

Hank's outside demeanor reflected a deeper and much more tragic reality. In no way was Hank changing. But here's what is most remarkable – Hank's fellow believers were not surprised by this.

Nobody called an emergency meeting to consider this strange case of a follower of Jesus who was not changing. You see, no one really expected Hank to change, so no one was surprised when it didn't happen.

> People did not expect that day by day, month by month, decade by decade, Hank would become more like Jesus. People did not expect that he would become a progressively more loving, joyful and pleasant person. So they weren't shocked when it didn't happen.

Discipleship is both an invitation and a challenge. Initially, Jesus invites people to simply come to Him. Once they respond to His grace, He starts training them to become like Him. As our relationship with God deepens, we begin to understand that following Jesus is a lifestyle of continual learning and personal change.

While God's specific approach varies from person to person, it is always spiritual and progressive. Jesus accepts people as they are, but He has no intention of leaving them that way. His influence in our lives will be nothing short of an extreme makeover – a makeover that changes us from what *we are* to what *Jesus is*. This requires time because we must be re-trained. God's training is spiritual, not academic. He deals with our hearts, not our heads.

Jesus personally invited and developed the twelve apostles (the apostles were chosen leaders). During their three years together, Jesus communicated both grace and progressive expectations. Jesus expected them to give up their fishing business so that they could learn to be *fishers of men* (Peter, Andrew, James and John were fishermen).

He expected them to form an attachment to Him that was actually stronger than their own family relationships. He expected them to be available to go wherever God would send them. Since Jesus hasn't changed, His expectations haven't changed. There is essentially no difference between what Jesus expected of His followers then, and what He expects of us today.

How Change Happens

God changes people from the inside. He changes people by changing their character. Spiritual development takes time. You can become a Christian in a moment – but not a *mature* one. A wedding ceremony is over in an hour. Building a strong marriage requires years. Likewise, the initial decision to trust Jesus is followed by a lifetime of learning and adjustment.

Becoming like Jesus is not something people achieve by themselves. People change through God's power and their participation. Personal change begins with the presence of the Holy Spirit. Through the Holy Spirit, Jesus comes to live in us. By His Spirit, God begins to write His laws – His *code of behavior* on our hearts.

Through His indwelling Holy Spirit, we learn what God wants us to do, stop doing, or do differently. God lovingly works in us and on us to transform our character.

The process of being transformed into the likeness of Jesus is called *sanctification*. The basic meaning of sanctification is to *make holy*. As the temple in the Old Testament was set apart as a holy place, now you are set apart as the temple where the Holy Spirit dwells. His role is to make you holy, because God is holy. Our job is to yield ourselves to His direction.

When a person receives Jesus into his heart, he is *born again*. Spiritual new birth is called *regeneration*. In regeneration, we pass *out of death into life*. On-going spiritual development is called *sanctification*. In sanctification, we pass *out of ourselves into Christ*. A person's *birth* is marked by a specific day. A person's *growth* is measured by development over years. In Scripture, our spiritual new birth happens when we initially *receive the Holy Spirit*. Spiritual growth involves continually *filling* our hearts with God's Word and Spirit.

Supernatural Work of the Holy Spirit

When the Spirit of God comes into a human heart it is a supernatural experience. Throughout Scripture, the activity of the Holy Spirit is described in different ways. Sincere followers of Jesus sometimes disagree on how to understand the work of God's Spirit in the souls of men. These Bible verses help us recognize how the Holy Spirit relates to people. The Holy Spirit...

- Prepares — Luke 4:1-2
- Refreshes — John 7:38
- Convicts — John 16:8
- Teaches — John 14:26
- Empowers — Luke 24:49
- Baptizes — Acts 1:5; 11:16
- Is a Gift — Acts 2:38; 5:32
- Fills — Acts 2:4; 4:31
- Selects — Acts 13:2
- Leads — Romans 8:14
- Intercedes — Romans 8:26
- Inhabits — I Corinthians 6:19
- Transforms — II Corinthians 3:18

Regardless of how God's people use and apply these concepts, the main emphasis of Scripture is clear: God wants to supernaturally **indwell, fill, transform, strengthen and guide our lives.** This new life begins when the Holy Spirit enters your heart.

In general, the New Testament teaches that the *gift* of the Holy Spirit comes to people when they receive the Lord Jesus by believing in His name. The apostle Peter said, *Repent and be baptized in the name of Jesus Christ so that your sins may be forgiven. And you will receive the gift of the Holy Spirit* (Acts 2:38). The apostle Paul wrote, *because you are sons, God sent the Spirit of His Son into our hearts* (Galatians 4:6).

Once this initial gift has been received, believers are exhorted to *be filled with the Spirit* (Ephesians 5:18). In other words, now that Jesus lives in you, let His Spirit fill you.

The initial gift of God's Spirit is a singular occurrence. Being filled with God's Spirit is not. The Spirit's fullness is not a once-for-all experience, but a privilege to be renewed continuously through trust and obedience.

Regarding God's Spirit, there are many fillings. When we initially confess our sins and believe, we *receive* the Holy Spirit. As we continue to surrender our lives we are *filled* with the Holy Spirit. Christ's followers should ask God for a fresh out-pouring of His Spirit every day.

Full of the Holy Spirit

Being full of the Holy Spirit allows Christ Himself to be Lord of your entire life. It means Jesus is indwelling *and* enthroned. This happens in the heart. It is not a physical or psychological experience, but rather a deeply spiritual one. Being filled with the Spirit allows God to govern your mind, emotions and will.

To fill something means to put in as much as possible. It means to occupy wholly. If a hotel is full, there is no vacancy. All the rooms are taken – all the rooms are occupied. If you picture your life as a hotel, God's Spirit wants to occupy every room.

Are you currently giving Jesus access to every room in your heart? Are there any rooms that are off limits? **Jesus doesn't live in us just to observe us.** He wants to occupy our whole personality so that we reflect His likeness. When Christ fills every part of your life, there is no vacancy for anything else. There is no room for Satan, the world or self.

Being filled with the Holy Spirit is God's will. *Do not get drunk with wine, which leads to debauchery. Instead, be filled with the Spirit* (Ephesians 5:18). Drinking to excess leads to drunkenness. When a person subjects his body to alcohol, he is under the influence of the alcohol he consumes. If he is drunk, the alcohol has full possession of him. His behavior reveals that he is *filled* with too much wine.

In contrast, when a person submits himself to the Spirit of God, he is under the influence of God. God's Spirit has taken full possession of his mind, emotions and will. His behavior reveals that he is under the direction of God's Spirit. This is what Jesus wants.

The visible result of being filled with the Spirit is reflecting the likeness of Jesus. *The fruit of the Spirit is love, joy, peace, patience, kindness, goodness, faithfulness, gentleness and self control* (Galatians 5:22). When we are filled with the Spirit, others see Christ in our lives.

The apostle Paul prayed that believers would be strengthened through God's Spirit for one purpose: *that you will be filled with all the measure of the fullness of God* (Ephesians 3:19). Paul prayed that Jesus would not only be *in* their lives, but that He would *fill* their lives.

Continuous Outpourings

The atoning work of Christ's death was once for all. However, the fresh power of God's Spirit is not given in a once-for-all method. The outpourings of God's Spirit are intended to be frequent and continuous. In his book, *Paths to Power,* A. W. Tozer writes,

> A disinterested observer, reading without the handicap of doctrinal prejudice, would surely gather from the Scriptures that God desires to advance his work among men by frequent outpourings of the Spirit upon his people as they need them and are prepared to receive them.
>
> In brief, the teaching of the New Testament is that the outpouring at Pentecost was the historic ***beginning of an era*** that was to be characterized by a continuous outpouring of the Holy Spirit.
>
> Through the prophet Joel, God had promised that He would, during the last days, pour out his Spirit upon all flesh. The phrase "the last days" applies to a period beginning with the first coming of Christ and continuing through His second.

The Scriptures teach that following the original outpouring of the Holy Spirit in Acts 2, God continued to shower the first century church with power from on high. Believers were *filled* with the Spirit of God in Acts 4, 6, 8, 9, 10, 13 and 19.

The lesson for us to learn is this: God's promise of power for His people is meant for the entire time Christ's Church is on earth. As long as the Church exists, she is to experience continual outpourings of the Holy Spirit.

In short, the book of Acts is an unfinished book, and in every generation God's people are to cry out to Him for a fresh anointing of His presence and power. Consider the example of Stephen, the first martyr in church history. Because of his receptive heart, God continued to fill his life.

Acts 6:3	Brothers, choose seven men from among you who are known to be *full* of the Spirit and wisdom.
Acts 6:5	They chose Stephen, a man *full* of faith and of the Holy Spirit.
Acts 7:55	But Stephen, *full* of the Holy Spirit, looked up to heaven and saw the glory of God, and Jesus standing at the right hand of God.

How to Be Filled with the Spirit

God wants us to be filled with His Spirit. There is, however, **no biblical formula** for how to be filled with the Holy Spirit. Without a prescribed "how to" formula, God usually prepares our hearts through personal difficulty. God wants to break our preoccupation with earthly things so that our attention is upon Him.

Experiencing God's fullness is not complicated when the conditions are correct. In general, the spiritual conditions that assist God's Spirit are contained in the words: *surrender, ask* and *obey.*

Surrender

The apostle Paul urged believers to *offer your bodies as living sacrifices, holy and pleasing to God. Do not conform any longer to the pattern of this world, but be transformed by the renewing of your mind* (Romans 12:1-2). Before God can fill us with Himself, we must first be emptied of ourselves. There must be a spirit of *forsaking* and *surrender.* We must be willing to abandon the outcome to God. Confessing past sins is often easier than letting go of future plans. Put your trust in God, not in how you think life should turn out.

Ask

Jesus said, *if you then, though you are evil, know how to give good gifts to your children, how much more will your Father in heaven give the Holy Spirit to those who ask him* (Luke 11:13). It is unlikely that God fills anyone with His Spirit who does not desire to be filled. In the Bible, those filled with God's Spirit wanted to be. To know God was the all-absorbing desire of their lives. Not only did they want to be wholly possessed by God, they *needed* to be.

Obey

God's Spirit does not fill an unwilling or disobedient heart. Peter said, *we are witnesses of these things, and so is the Holy Spirit which God has given to those who obey him* (Acts 5:32). Complete and ungrudging obedience to the will of God is absolutely indispensable to the reception of the Spirit's fresh anointing. Zechariah was disciplined for not embracing the angel's announcement regarding the name of his son. When he obeyed God by naming his son John, he was immediately filled with the Holy Spirit (Luke 1:67).

In his book, *When God Comes to Church,* Ray Ortlund tells the story of Jeremy Bentham, a millionaire who died in 1832. Jeremy Bentham willed his estate to the University College Hospital in London, on one bizarre condition. He required that his dead body be dissected and then his skeleton re-assembled, preserved, and clothed so that he could *attend* all subsequent board meetings of the hospital.

To this day, dressed in his nineteenth-century attire, Jeremy Bentham is wheeled into the hospital's board meetings and the chairman pronounces, "Jeremy Bentham, present but not voting." The reality for many believers is that Jesus is present but not voting. The only way others will be convinced that our gospel is true is if Jesus is in charge of the way we live our lives.

Process *and* Crisis

Jesus wants His disciples to be like Him. *A student is not above his teacher, but everyone who is fully trained will be like his teacher* (Luke 6:40). The process of becoming like Christ is both a spiritual crisis and a progressive experience. Simply put, there are seasons when our spiritual growth is gradual. There are other times when we experience a sudden personal revelation from God. *Crisis* does not mean tragedy. Crisis moments are personal revelations from God Himself. In these teachable moments, God suddenly opens our eyes. The spiritual experience is a milestone because it marks a significant turning point in our lives. Throughout history, Jesus has shaped His followers through both crisis moments and progressive experiences.

The founder of the *Christian and Missionary Alliance,* A. B. Simpson, was raised by a strict Presbyterian father. Simpson started preaching at age twenty-two in Canada. His second pastorate was eight years later in Kentucky. It was during this ministry that he began to recognize his need to be filled with the Spirit of God.

The churches in Kentucky had become deeply divided during the years of the Civil War. Simpson's goal was to pull the divided denominations together. Every age had their "big name" preachers. In Simpson's day, it was Major Whittle and songwriter, Philip Bliss (Philip Bliss wrote the song, *It is Well with My Soul).* In A. W. Tozer's biography of A. B. Simpson, he explains how Simpson was powerfully transformed by God:

> Up to this time Simpson had very much been a church man, visualizing the whole religious picture as an adventure in respectability. He had been willing to slave his heart out within the proper framework of approved church activities, but generally nothing more.
>
> It is remarkable how great a man can be, how faithfully he can labor in the gospel ministry, how much he can appear to accomplish in the work of the church and still be far short of the rich, power-driven service possible to the Spirit-filled servants of God.
>
> Mr. Simpson began to see this plainly and the knowledge was not comforting to him. Until he came into contact with Major Whittle, he had not realized how much pride and self there was within him, and how little the power of Christ.
>
> There was something about Major Whittle, some overtone of power, some fragrance of Christ, some hovering Presence that melted the brilliant young Presbyterian minister like a vision of God. A thousand flaws appeared to him, galling, painful, Christ dishonoring. He must have more of God – he must be filled with the Spirit.
>
> The time appears to have been some days after the close of the Whittle meetings. There in the privacy of his own room with no one to understand or sympathize, his Gethsemane came to him. He yielded himself to God in utter surrender. From that hour he was turned into another man. He would live from that time on, in his own words, a consecrated, crucified and Christ-devoted life.

This was A. B. Simpson's spiritual crisis. It was a sudden personal revelation from God to his heart. Through this encounter, Simpson recognized that something was missing. While he may have had all of the Holy Spirit, the Holy Spirit did not have all of him. God opened his eyes to see his *self-life* – all that was hindering the Holy Spirit's work in his life.

Has the Lord been preparing you for just such a turning point in your life? Do you want to be filled with God's Spirit more than you want anything else?

Would you like to have a heart that reflects the character of Jesus? Are you ready to surrender your personality to the One who made and bought you?

Jesus stands ready to take over the management of your life. Are you willing to give Him everything you naturally call your own – your marriage, children, career? Will you abandon the outcome to God?

If the answer to these questions is *yes,* God will lead you through your own Gethsemane and transform you into another person. In the end, you will experience an extreme makeover.

Individual Response Questions

1. Why does becoming like Jesus take time?

2. How does being *filled* with the Spirit differ from initially *receiving* the Holy Spirit?

3. If your life is like a hotel, what are some of the *rooms* the Holy Spirit wants to occupy?

4. Describe a time when your spiritual growth happened suddenly.

5. To draw closer to God, which spiritual condition (surrender, ask, obey) should you pursue?

6. What part of this lesson was most meaningful to you?

Personal Assessment

On a scale from 1-6, circle your response (1 means *not true* of you; 6 means *is true* of you).

- I sincerely want my character to be transformed.

  1 2 3 4 5 6

- I am daily aware that God is working in me and on me.

  1 2 3 4 5 6

- I see the visible effect of the Holy Spirit in my life. I am becoming more like Christ.

  1 2 3 4 5 6

- I am repenting of behavior that demonstrates that Jesus is *present but not voting*.

  1 2 3 4 5 6

- I offer to God my future plans.

  1 2 3 4 5 6

Lesson 10 – Show Me the Power

§

In Over your Head

My daughter Carey began her work as a nurse in Mali, West Africa, in September 2005. Before she left, I asked her to recommend a book that would help me understand her life in Africa. She handed me a very "comforting" book entitled, *Before We Kill and Eat You*.

The book describes the true life story of Henry and Ruth Garlock who were pioneer missionaries to Liberia in 1920. One of the common experiences the Garlocks encountered was various African tribes who had many deep superstitions.

These superstitions were evident by the *fetish charms* they wore around their necks or waists, and hung above the doorways of their huts. By wearing these charms on their bodies, people believed they would be protected from wild animals, hostile tribes and sickness.

One village had a very large fetish at its main entrance. It was a large structure in the form of an arch. Everyone who entered the village passed under it. Ironically, at the other entrance to the same village was a Christian mission station.

Eventually, Henry pointed out to the chief of the tribe that it didn't look right to have a fetish shrine at one end and a Christian mission at the other. He proceeded to put the chief on the spot by telling him about Elijah challenging the priests of Baal on Mt. Carmel. He even quoted Elijah's words, "How long will you waver between two opinions? If the Lord is God follow him; but if Baal is God follow him."

Henry writes,

> My challenge was premature. As long as I live I shall never forget the chief's reply.
>
> "White man, you have asked us to give up the religion of our ancestors for a new religion, one that has not been tried by our people. You tell us that your God has all power – that he can cleanse the leper, open the eyes of the blind and raise the dead. You have just told us about Elijah's God sending down fire from heaven. But we have not seen any fire, or any power of the God you talk about.
>
> We are prepared to consider serving your God, but before doing so we would like to see a demonstration of this power you are talking about. There are many lepers in our village – would you mind healing some of them? There are many blind among us. Please heal some of these. And our people are dying every day.
>
> As soon as we witness some of the miracles you have preached about take place among our people, we will consider destroying the big fetish as you suggest."

Henry vowed he would never preach in the village again until God did something. For days, he prayed and lay on his face before the Lord. He asked the school children living on the compound to join him in fasting and prayer.

One child who attended the mission school was the son of the chief. James was a 12-year-old boy who was almost blind from cataracts on his eyes. After hearing how Jesus healed a blind man named Bartimaeus, James asked, "Do you think Jesus is able to heal my eyes?"

After what had taken place in town a few weeks before, Henry knew that this was his opportunity to seek God's power. He told James to cry out to God with all his heart. Henry writes,

> James knelt down and cried out to God with all his might – I suppose much as blind Bartimaeus had done at Jericho. When I knew James meant business, I knelt down beside him and laid my hands upon his eyes. I asked God, for Jesus' sake, for the sake of James' father and for the sake of the people in the tribe who had asked to see a miracle of God's power, to please heal this boy.

> Suddenly James opened his eyes and looked up. I could see that the cataracts had completely disappeared – his eyes were clear. His face lit up, and without saying a word he jumped to his feet, dashed out the door of the chapel and ran all the way to town to his father's house to show him what God had done.
>
> The murky film that had covered his eyes was gone and the boy could see. Because he was the son of the chief, news of his healing soon spread throughout the entire village.

Henry Garlock suddenly realized he didn't have what it took. He got down on his face and said in effect, *"Lord, I'm in over my head."* There are some moments where mere words are not the solution. John Stott writes,

> Authentic Christianity – the Christianity of Christ and his apostles – is supernatural Christianity. It is not a tame and harmless ethic, consisting of a few moral platitudes, spiced with a dash of religion. It is resurrection religion, a life lived by the power of God.

Try Harder

Ray Stedman told the story of a husband and wife who were professional counselors. After they became followers of Jesus they realized there was a difference between secular counseling (solving problems using the world's approach) and spiritual counseling (solving problems by looking to God). Based on their new understanding, they changed their approach.

One day a new client came into their office. Before the session began the counselors said, "In our practice, we offer two types of counseling. We offer secular counseling and spiritual counseling. Which would you prefer?"

The client said, "Well, I have never been a religious person. So, if it's just the same to you I'd like to have the secular counseling." The counselors replied, "No problem, just sit down, relax and tell us all about your situation."

For the next two hours the man poured out his heart. He revealed every secret, every struggle and every fear. He told them how unsuccessful he felt up to this point. He totally bared his soul in hopes of finding a solution. At the end of the session he was exhausted. He quietly waited for some professional insight and a ray of hope.

The counselors casually leaned forward and looked the man straight in the eye. "We believe we know the solution for your problems."

"After listening to my story one time, you really know what I should do?"

"Yes, we want you to try harder."

The client couldn't believe his ears. "Try harder," he scowled, "what kind of advice is that?" The counselors repeated themselves. "You heard us! Given your situation you must try harder! Bear down! Put out more effort! WE WANT YOU TO TRY HARDER!"

The client was outraged. He demanded an explanation. "What kind of answer is that?" The counselors quietly replied, "You told us that you wanted *secular* counseling, didn't you? Well, that's the secular answer – try harder."

"What if I said that I wanted *spiritual* counseling?"

"Well then, we would have told you to *trust Christ*. Given your set of problems, you have two options: try harder or trust Christ. You can use your own tiny will power or you can turn to Jesus and learn to depend on His divine power. There are only two sources of power available in the world today: *yours* and *His*. The one you depend on is up to you."

Qualities of Spiritual Power

Spiritual power produces courageous followers. Men and women of courage understand *following* to mean the established habit of obedience to the commandments of Christ. They recognize that God works as long as His people live daringly. The power of God comes only when the followers of Jesus are doing something that requires it.

Spiritual power produces worshipers. These followers are more devoted to Jesus than an institution. Their loyalty is to God, not human personalities. They live for God's glory.

Spiritual power produces genuine holiness. When the mysterious and unexplainable presence of God is real, the world takes note. In the first century, the regard for Christ's followers was so high that nobody but true believers dared to join them (Acts 5:13). No comment could be more hurtful to a follower of Jesus than, "You are no different from anybody else."

Spiritual power produces a passion for non-followers. Spirit-empowered people are never *settled* – they are constantly on the move. *God anointed Jesus of Nazareth with the Holy Spirit and power and he went around doing good* (Acts 10:38). They are possessed by a passion for people to know the love of God. They know that life is no longer all about them.

Spiritual power makes Jesus' Kingdom real. Followers of Jesus are known for their access to a power source that the world does not know. *Then the disciples went out and preached everywhere, and the Lord worked with them and confirmed his word by the signs that accompanied it* (Mark 16:20). When kingdom people pray, God intervenes. Changed lives are living proof that Christ's gospel is true.

Someone once said, *It's not the lofty sails that move the ship, but the unseen wind.* Just as a sail needs the power of the wind, we need the power of the Holy Spirit.

All things being equal, followers of Jesus will have as much success in the Lord's work as they have power – no more and no less. Spiritual obstacles and difficult circumstances may hinder for a time, but nothing can stand against the raw power of God.

God Has the Power

In the book of Acts, we learn that true Christianity is the continuation of the life of Christ. Jesus is the original founder and current head of His work in the world. The kingdom of God is not a specific denomination or a religious club, but rather a *spiritual movement.*

This movement is not based on buildings, programs or personalities. Christ promised His followers, *I am going to send you what my Father has promised; but stay in the city until you have been clothed with power from on high* (Luke 24:49). For the super-human task of making disciples of all nations, Jesus promised supernatural power.

Interestingly, the word *love* is not found one time in the book of Acts. We can only wonder why – especially since Jesus promised, *all men would know that you are my disciples if you love one another* (John 13:35). The early followers of Jesus were loving people. However, the key to their success was not merely their humanitarian concern. Human kindness can only go so far. The kingdom of God expands because Jesus provides the power to make it grow. **It's not the lofty sails that move the ship, but the unseen wind.**

Jesus wants His followers to be conscious of His presence and to depend on His power. To experience spiritual power in our own lives, we must confidently believe that God can handle whatever situation we are facing. Nothing is too difficult for God.

Good News and Bad News

Perhaps the most famous story in the Old Testament is the episode of God calling Moses to lead the children of Israel out of slavery in Egypt, and into the Promised Land (around 1270 BC). To accomplish this, Pharaoh, the ruler of the Egyptians, had to be convinced to let approximately one million Hebrew slaves go. Understandably, he did not want to do this.

It was God's power that influenced his decision. The Bible says that God sent ten plagues upon the land of Egypt. These plagues were designed to demonstrate God's supremacy and convince Pharaoh to surrender to God's plan.

Eventually Pharaoh relented and God led the Israelites out of Egypt. They quickly arrived at the Red Sea. At this juncture, Pharaoh changed his mind and decided to pursue the Israelites. With the Red Sea in front of them and the Egyptian army coming behind them, God parted the waters of the Red Sea so that the Israelites could walk across on dry land.

When the Egyptian army tried to pursue them, God released the waters and the Egyptian army drowned in the sea. Clearly, God's miraculous power delivered them from slavery.

A few months later, Moses sent leaders from the people to look over the land that the Lord had promised to give them. For forty days, twelve men explored the land. What happened next was a turning point for over one million people. The focus of this moment was one question: **Is God able to do what He promised?**

When the twelve men returned, the people heard two entirely different reports. Ten men brought back *bad news* and two men brought back *good news*.

The ten men who delivered a negative report said in effect, "True, it is a land flowing with milk and honey – but you can forget it. They have very powerful people, fortified cities and giants!" *We seemed like grasshoppers in our own eyes, and we looked the same to them* (Numbers 13:33).

But Joshua and Caleb, the two men who trusted the Lord wholeheartedly, said *if the Lord is pleased with us, He will lead us into the land. Don't be afraid of them; their protection is gone. The Lord is with us* (Numbers 14:8-9).

What is so amazing is that *all* twelve men saw exactly the same set of circumstances. The ten men who brought back a negative report saw the overwhelming circumstances – and nothing else. They tried to convince the people that taking possession of the land was impossible. Even though they saw all ten plagues and the parting of the Red Sea, somehow this situation was different.

By contrast, Joshua and Caleb saw both the circumstances *and* the power of God. They told the people that there would definitely be a fight, but with God leading them they would surely win. Nothing is greater than God's power. God is able to do what He promised!

Picture in a Picture

Several years ago, I was strolling through a furniture store and for the first time I saw a television set with *a picture in a picture*. One picture was large – it filled up the entire screen. The other picture was small – it was placed in the upper-left corner.

This television reminded me of the experience of the twelve spies who explored the Promised Land. Ten men saw nothing but giants and fortified cities. To them, these problems were large. They filled the entire screen. God's power was small – like the little picture in the corner.

To Joshua and Caleb, it was God's power that filled the entire screen. The problem of the giants and fortified cities was like the smaller picture in the upper-left corner. In our own lives we face similar situations.

As you look at your circumstances today, which is the big picture – God's power or your problem? Is your problem the small picture in the corner? Or is God's power the small picture? Just like the twelve men, our perspective of God's ability will influence our faith.

The Hebrew people became discouraged and started to complain. They lost confidence in God. *We should have died in Egypt, or at least the desert. Our wives and children will be taken as slaves. We should choose a leader and go back to Egypt* (Numbers 14:2-4). God viewed their unbelief as a personal insult.

Except for Joshua, Caleb, and their families, every adult age twenty and older, was not allowed to enter the Promised Land. They forfeited their reward on earth because they lost confidence in God's power and ability. **When we forget what God has done, we forget what God can do.** When we remember what God has done, we realize what God can do. It's not the lofty sails that move the ship, but the unseen wind.

What Are the Odds?

In the summer of 1996, Peggy was diagnosed with breast cancer. After the surgery, the surgeon said to me, "Look, I want to tell it like it is. There are a number of complicating factors here and the odds aren't that good that she will live five years."

The notion of *her odds* stayed with me for some time. One day while I was praying, I remember having a conversation with God about *Peggy's odds*. A turning point in my life came when God spoke to my heart, "Paul, I don't care what the odds are. I never consider the odds."

What were the odds of the Israelites being able to destroy the giants in the land of Canaan? Humanly speaking, they weren't very good; but we're not talking about human power – we're talking about God's power. God's power is resurrection power. It has been noted that resurrection power is reserved for graveyards. Resurrection power only works when the situation looks hopeless. Resurrection power is for people facing impossible odds. God's power can heal bodies, relationships and finances. Nothing is impossible with God. **He never considers the odds.**

God Empowers People

The foundation for experiencing God's power is to be fully convinced that God has the power. The next step is to believe that **God can empower you!** *God is able to do immeasurably more than all we ask or imagine according to His power that is at work within us* (Ephesians 3:20).

You are God's representative. As His representative, God expresses His authority and power through you. God supplies the power; you provide the means. Consider these examples:

Moses — *Moses stretched out his hand over the sea...and all night the Lord drove back the sea with a strong east wind* (Exodus 14:21).

David — *David said to the Philistine, "You come against me with sword and spear and javelin, but I come against you in the name of the Lord Almighty...it is not by sword or spear that the Lord saves; for the battle is the Lord's, and he will give you into our hands"* (I Samuel 17:45; 47).

Mary — *But the angel said to her, "Do not be afraid, Mary, you have found favor with God. You will be with child and give birth to a son, and you are to give him the name Jesus. The Holy Spirit will come upon you; and the power of the Most High will over-shadow you"* (Luke 1:31; 35).

It is clear that *through* Moses, God led His people out of Egypt. *Through* David, God killed the giant Goliath. God brought Jesus into the world *through* Mary. Today, Christ continues to impact the world *through* us. Jesus supplies the power – His followers provide the means.

Flashlight, Pen & Glove

Why does a flashlight need a battery to produce light? It was made that way. The presence of the battery within the flashlight is indispensable to its ability to function as it was intended. Have you ever tried to use a flashlight that didn't have a battery? It doesn't work. The power of the Holy Spirit is as indispensable to us as a battery is to a flashlight.

Why does a pen need ink in order to write? It was made that way. The presence of the ink within the pen is indispensable to its ability to function as it was intended. Have you ever tried to write with a pen that was out of ink? It doesn't work. The power of the Holy Spirit is as indispensable to us as ink is to a pen.

Why does a glove need a hand in order to pick something up? It was made that way. The presence of the hand within the glove is indispensable to its ability to function as it was intended. Have you ever tried to order a glove to pick something up by itself? It doesn't work. However, as soon as a hand comes into the glove, the glove becomes as strong as the hand. Everything that is possible for the hand becomes possible for the glove. You are the *glove* and Christ is the *hand.*

The Father *Through* the Son

Jesus is God. He is the First and the Last; the Beginning and the End. All things were made by Him and for Him. Jesus has always been God and will always be God, but for thirty-three years Jesus became a man. However, Jesus was man as God intended. He was a sinless man.

The Bible teaches that when Jesus became a human being, although He was God, He surrendered His divine power and privilege. *Who, being in the very nature God, did not consider equality with God something to be grasped, but made himself nothing, taking the very nature of a servant, and being made in human likeness* (Philippians 2:6-7).

During Jesus' earthly life, He offered himself completely to His Father. *When Christ entered the world he said, "Sacrifices and offerings you have not desired, but a body you have prepared for me. Then I said, 'Here I am. I have come to do your will, O God'"* (Hebrews 10:5-7). The Father could do His work through His Son because Jesus was fully available and totally dependent.

During His ministry, Jesus explained that the miracles people saw were the result of the Father's power working *through* Him. In other words, His Father was the *battery* – Jesus was the *flashlight*. His Father was the *hand* – Jesus was the *glove*.

If we can discover how the Father did His work through the Son, we will discover how Jesus intends to do His work through us. Jesus constantly taught that His power did not come from Himself but rather from His Father. This amazing spiritual principle is revealed again and again.

John 5:19	The Son can do nothing by himself; he can only do what he sees his Father doing.
John 5:30	By myself I can do nothing.
John 7:16	My teaching is not my own. It comes from him who sent me.
John 14:9-10	The words I say to you are not just my own. Rather it is the Father living in me who is doing His work.
Acts 2:22	Jesus of Nazareth was a man accredited by God to you by miracles, wonders and signs, which God did among you through him.

JESUS *THROUGH* US

Most ordinary activities are initiated by the mind. Our work is directed by our mind through the members of our bodies. As the Head, Christ directs the work of the Church through the members of His body. **The ministry of Jesus is what He does through us, not what we do for Him.** Jesus said, *I will build my church* (Matthew 16:18). Christ Himself promised to build His Church on earth and He is fully competent to build it *through us*.

Jesus is alive and in charge. He is undefeatable and unstoppable. All power in heaven and earth belong to Him. We must credit Him with having enough intelligence to know what He's doing. If you are capable of directing the activity of your body, don't you think Jesus is capable of directing the activity of His?

Can you imagine your hand forming a *get-things-picked-up-committee* with all of your fingers? What if they met every morning to create a strategic plan of what they are going to do for you? Now imagine multiple committees composed of your eyes, ears and feet, all doing the same thing. The result would be chaotic.

As the one in charge of your body, you know exactly what needs to be done. You simply need the members of your body to be available and dependent. Christ needs the same thing from the members of His body.

You are the Site

When A. B. Simpson lived in New York City, he told a story about a millionaire. This very rich man was looking for a special piece of ground to build a new house. He noticed that in the upper portion of the city there were some choice sites of land. Unfortunately, these sites were already taken by a number of very poor people. Little shacks were littered everywhere.

Simpson said, "The shacks were unworthy of the land on which they sat." One day, the millionaire approached the owner of one of those shacks and offered to buy the site. The current owner agreed, but on one condition.

"Give me some time to fix it up. It needs a new roof and a fresh coat of paint."

The millionaire smiled and responded, "My friend, I don't want an old, poorly built wreck of a house, even if it was repaired. I would never live in a place like that. All I want is the site – the location. All I am looking for is the ground. After I buy it I will turn your old shack into rubbish and then I will build my own new mansion according to my magnificent plans. No, I don't want your old house. All I want is the location."

Today, Jesus is looking for a site for a heavenly temple on earth – and you are that site! All Jesus wants is a location, a special place for His Spirit to dwell, fill and empower – and you are the location. He doesn't need any form of self-improvement or a promise to try harder. All Jesus wants is to **live** in you and **work** through you.

Jesus has put His Spirit into your heart and added you to His body. Jesus now clothes His divine activity with your redeemed humanity. You are His chosen instrument. Jesus now has your physical body with which to work. He has your mind, heart, eyes, ears, lips, feet and hands. He intends to continue His work through you.

Individual Response Questions

1. What is the difference between *trying harder* and *trusting Christ?*

2. Which characteristics of spiritual power are most lacking in Christ's followers today?

3. After crossing the Red Sea so quickly, why did the Israelites forget the power of God?

4. In what ways did Jesus depend upon God's power?

5. What life experiences have taught you to depend on God's power?

6. What part of this lesson was most meaningful to you?

Personal Assessment

On a scale from 1-6, circle your response (1 means *not true* of you; 6 means *is true* of you).

- I behave with the assurance that God has the power to handle what concerns me today.

  1 2 3 4 5 6

- In a difficult situation, I quickly turn to God. I rely on His resources.

  1 2 3 4 5 6

- Because I trust in God's power, I seldom worry.

  1 2 3 4 5 6

- I consider myself a courageous, holy believer with a passion for people.

  1 2 3 4 5 6

- I am depending upon God's power more today than I did a year ago.

  1 2 3 4 5 6

Lesson 11 – Everyone's Vulnerable

§

Trapped

On August 12, 2000, the Kursk, a Russian nuclear submarine carrying 118 crewmembers, sank in the Barents Sea. The Russian government insisted that the entire crew died within minutes of the explosion. Six weeks later the world learned the truth. Very soon after the explosion, SOS signals in Morse code were heard.

Russian naval officer Dmitry Kolesnikov wrote a letter after he and twenty-three other crewmembers survived the initial explosion. The letter was written to his wife, Olga, whom he had recently married.

An article in *Newsweek* on November 6, 2000 revealed the content of the note. The note began with neat, cursive handwriting, suggesting the lights were still on:

> All the crew from the 6th, 7th, and 8th compartments went over to the 9th. There are twenty-three people here. We have made this decision as a result of the accident. None of us can get to the surface.

On the back of the paper, the writing is smudged, nearly illegible, apparently suggesting that the lights had gone out. "I am writing blind," Kolesnikov scribbled. He wrapped the letter in plastic and put it into his pocket where a Russian diver found it.

This tragic event provides a powerful illustration of the devastation that sin can cause. The submarine wasn't attacked from without – something failed from within. The survivors felt trapped. Their final days were characterized by panic and hopelessness. None of them could get to the surface on their own.

The toll sin takes on our lives is multi-faceted. Sin triggers a chain reaction. Initially, the fall-out is a troubled conscience and feelings of guilt. If those warning signs are ignored, rationalization takes over. If disobedience persists, a sense of powerlessness sets in.

In the end, you feel trapped. You begin doubting your relationship with God. You wonder, "I know I need help, but who can I trust? Who would befriend me in this condition?" It's a serious mistake to assume that this could not happen to you. Everyone's vulnerable.

A Universal Reality

In the model prayer, Jesus taught us to be on guard: *And lead us not into temptation, but deliver us from the evil one* (Matthew 6:13). Jesus knew the importance of being alert to the devil's tricks. In his book, *The Myth of the Greener Grass,* J. Allan Petersen writes,

> When you were born you were married – married to a companion who will walk the road of life with you until the end.
>
> You will never awaken any morning or retire any night without this companion being right at your side. This companion will never leave you for reasons of non-support. It is impossible to get a divorce.
>
> Whether you like it or not, you and this partner will be together until death do you part. *Temptation* – your lifelong companion.
>
> Everyone is tempted. Temptation knows no strangers. Everyone is tempted and always will be. No one can evade it or avoid it. It is an inescapable fact of life.
>
> If man is alive, he is tempted. No isolation from people will isolate us from temptation. There are no exceptions. No exemptions. Temptation is a universal, inevitable reality.

The devil is God's enemy. No matter how seemingly innocent the temptation appears to be, the devil's sole purpose is to ruin your life. The Bible likens Satan to five animals:

- *Serpent* – attempting to deceive all people (Genesis 3:1-6)
- *Bird* – trying to snatch God's Word from human hearts (Matthew 13:19)
- *Wolf* – attacking God's flock (John 10:12)
- *Lion* – seeking to devour God's children (I Peter 5:8)
- *Dragon* – wanting to destroy God's Son (Revelation 12:7)

It is important to acknowledge Satan's activity, but not be intimidated by him. God promises that the devil can be resisted and defeated.

James 4:7-8	Resist the devil and he will flee from you. Come near to God and He will come near to you.
I Corinthians 10:13	No temptation has seized you except what is common to man. But when you are tempted, He will also provide a way out so that you can stand up under it.
I John 4:4	The One who is in you is greater than the one who is in the world.

When A Believer Sins

You may ask, "What happens when a believer yields to temptation and sins? Does he forfeit his relationship with God and cease to be His child? John Stott responds to this question:

> No. Think of the analogy of a human family. A boy is offensively rude to his parents. A cloud descends on the home. There is tension in the atmosphere. Father and son are not on speaking terms. What has happened? Has the boy ceased to be a son? No. Their relationship hasn't changed; it is their fellowship that has been broken.
>
> Relationship depends on birth; fellowship depends on behavior. As soon as the boy apologizes, he is forgiven. And forgiveness restores fellowship. Meanwhile, his relationship remained the same. He may have been temporarily disobedient, or even defiant, but he has not ceased to be a son. So it is with God's children.

Every follower of Jesus is vulnerable to willful disobedience. This is not referring to losing one's salvation, but rather losing one's closeness to God. People who know, love and follow Jesus are still vulnerable to temptation, sin and personal failure. This includes brand new believers as well as mature, seasoned leaders.

God helps us resist temptation. *No temptation has seized you except what is common to man. And God is faithful; He will not let you be tempted beyond what you can bear. But when you are tempted, He will also provide a way out so that you can stand up under it* (I Corinthians 10:13).

Even though God provides a way out, His people don't always make the right choice. It is naïve to think that we will encounter a believer who has *never* become entrapped by sin. It can happen to any of us. The apostle Peter was certain that he would never deny the Lord. *Peter insisted emphatically, "Even if I have to die with you, I will never disown you"* (Mark 14:31).

Like Peter, we all have preconceived ideas of what we would *never do*. Followers of Jesus need help in coping with paralyzing and disabling sins. If it's not you, it will be someone you know.

Help and Hope

In I John 2:1, the apostle John wrote these words to encourage believers.

> *My dear children, I write this to you so that you do not sin. But if anybody does sin, we have one who speaks to the Father in our defense – Jesus Christ, the Righteous One.*

If we sin, who besides Jesus will come to our defense? Fallen followers need help and hope. Specifically, they need compassion and guidance. They need to know that God still loves them and people still believe in them.

Jesus was never surprised or caught off-guard by personal failure. Rather, he sympathized with the one who failed. In the same way, God wants *mature followers* to reach out to the fallen with mercy and truth.

God wants *fallen followers* to come to terms with their behavior, turn their lives around, and not give up. *My brothers, if one of you should wander from the truth and someone should bring him back, remember this: Whoever turns a sinner away from his error will save him from death and cover a multitude of sins* (James 5:19-20).

In every era, God-fearing men and women have experienced huge personal failures. The Bible records the personal failures of many loyal followers, including well-known leaders such as Moses, David, Jonah and Peter.

These were people of faith. All believed in God and knew God. In a very real sense, all of these people had *a past.*

Moses was a murderer – but years later he received the Ten Commandments from God Himself and proclaimed to the people the eighth commandment: *You shall not murder* (Exodus 20:13).

David was an adulterer and a murderer – but he also had a future. He said, *I will teach transgressors your ways, and sinners will return to you* (Psalm 51:13).

Jonah deliberately ran from God – but a short time later he was used to warn the people of Nineveh of pending destruction (Jonah 3:3-10).

Peter denied knowing Jesus. But Peter's disgrace of denying the Lord three times did not derail God's plan for his future ministry (John 18 & 21).

Jesus loves us regardless. **Jesus never becomes disillusioned with people.** Jesus is not embarrassed to identify himself with "sinners." C. S. Lewis once said, "Think of me as a fellow-patient in the same hospital, who having been admitted a little earlier, could give some advice."

Let the testimonies of Moses, David, Jonah and Peter be your *fellow-patients* who were admitted a little earlier. Let the outcome of their lives be a voice that provides hope. If you are willing to face reality and surrender your future to God, you'll be moving in the right direction.

Devastating Sins

To God, all sin is sin. He never distinguishes between big and small sins. However, the **consequences** for different sins vary. Some sins are more devastating than others. Some sins bring greater shame. Solomon warned that some foolish choices bring public humiliation. *I have come to the brink of utter ruin in the midst of the whole assembly* (Proverbs 5:14). Devastating sins bring great shame upon God, others and ourselves.

Progressive Self-destruction

The Scripture teaches that God never tempts anyone to sin.

> *When tempted, no one should say, "God is tempting me." For God cannot be tempted by evil, nor does He tempt anyone; but each one is tempted when, by his own evil desire, he is dragged away and enticed. Then, after desire has conceived, it gives birth to sin; and sin, when it is full-grown, gives birth to death* (James 1:13-15).

The universal pathway to self-destruction is **desire – sin – death.** Personal failure is the result of personal choices.

Personal failure doesn't *just happen*. If someone self-destructs, it usually happens gradually. Sin is like a powerful drug. After the initial jolt you become progressively addicted until you lose the ability to break free. This leads to dangerous rationalizations. That is how sin becomes so lethal. Destructive thoughts can invade your heart, take root, and grow into habits that eventually control your behavior.

Judges 13-16 records the progressive downfall of a man named Samson. Samson's birth was miraculous because his mother was sterile and childless. God intended Samson *to begin the deliverance of Israel from the hands of the Philistines* (Judges 13:5).

The Philistines, a warlike people who settled along the coast of Palestine around 1200 BC, were one of Israel's principal rivals. God empowered Samson with unusual physical strength that came from being a Nazirite, set apart to God from birth. This is explained in Numbers 6:2-5.

> *If a man or woman wants to make a special vow, a vow of separation to the Lord as a Nazirite, he must abstain from wine and other fermented drink and must not drink vinegar made from wine or from other fermented drink. During the entire period of his vow of separation no razor may be used on his head. He must be holy until the period of his separation is over; he must let the hair of his head grow long.*

God commanded Samson's mother to follow this vow during her pregnancy. Samson also took this vow. His God-given physical strength was conditioned by this vow. Samson knew that if his head was shaved, his strength would be lost. He would become as weak as any other man.

Along the way, Samson fell in love with a godless woman named Delilah. The leaders of the Philistines approached Delilah and said, *See if you can lure him into showing you the secret of his great strength and how we can overpower him so we can tie him up and subdue him. Each one of us will give you eleven hundred shekels of silver* (Judges 16:5).

On three separate occasions Samson noticed that Delilah was trying to trick him and hand him over to the Philistines. Nevertheless, he kept spending time with her. Delilah said, *How can you say, 'I love you' when you won't confide in me? This is the third time you have made a fool of me and haven't told me the secret of your strength. With such nagging she prodded him day after day until he was tired to death* (Judges 16:15-16).

Finally Samson told her everything. Delilah put him to sleep on her lap and called a man to shave off his hair. His strength left him and the Philistines gouged out his eyes and put him in prison.

Samson slowly self-destructed. His downfall resulted from personal choices. He spent day after day in a compromising situation – with a woman he enjoyed being with. Eventually she ruined him. The story of Samson helps us understand why God warns us to guard against temptation. **Everyone is vulnerable.**

Ted Bundy

In his book, *Addicted to Love,* Stephen Arterburn writes about Ted Bundy's final interview with Dr. James Dobson, the Founder of *Focus on the Family.* Theodore R. "Ted" Bundy (1946-1989) was a serial murderer and rapist. He was one of the most notorious criminals in the late 20th century. Bundy confessed to twenty-eight killings, but other estimates indicate that he killed as many as thirty-three to one hundred female victims in the U.S. during the 1970's.

Outwardly, Ted Bundy appeared to be an example of a good, upstanding citizen. A one-time Boy Scout with a promising career in Washington state politics, Bundy was commended by Seattle police for saving the life of a three-year-old boy who was drowning in a lake.

But his life ended in an electric chair on January 24, 1989 at the State Penitentiary in Starke, Florida. Hours before his execution, Bundy called Dobson and offered the interview with the understanding that it would be used to warn the public of how his downfall actually took place.

Important points were made during the interview and then reinforced by direct Bundy quotes:

- BUNDY WAS NOT BORN A MONSTER. HE BEGAN LIFE AS A NORMAL PERSON

  There was no physical abuse or fighting in the home...I led a normal life.

- OBSCENITY IS PROGRESSIVELY ADDICTIVE

  You reach that jumping off point where you begin to wonder if maybe actually doing it will give you that which is beyond just reading about it or looking at it.

- THERE IS A CONNECTION BETWEEN OBSCENITY AND CRIMINAL BEHAVIOR

  I've met a lot of men who were motivated to commit violence just like me. And without exception, every one of them was deeply involved in pornography.

To illustrate his progressive self-destruction, Bundy said he began casually reading soft-core pornography when he was twelve or thirteen years old. He offered this final reflection on the impact pornography had on his life:

> Throughout the years, reading pornography became a deadly habit. I don't know why I was so vulnerable to it. All I know is pornography had an impact on me that was very central to the development of other violent behavior.
>
> Basically, I was a normal person. I wasn't some guy hanging out at bars. I wasn't someone you'd look at and say 'there's a pervert.' I had good friends. I led a normal life – except for one small but potent and destructive segment of it that I kept very secret and didn't let anybody know about.

We are most vulnerable when we think we're not. Which of these warning signs do you recognize in your life?

- Overestimating your own strength and capacity to resist temptation.
- Underestimating the deceptive power of Satan, the world and selfish desires.
- Developing an angry, bitter and critical spirit.
- Focusing on your rights and magnifying the faults of others.
- Shifting blame and responsibility on to others, life itself, and even God.
- Desiring to impress others and receive the applause that belongs to Christ alone.
- Refusing to make yourself accountable in the area of your greatest weakness.

Return to God

When you sin, God wants you to *repent*. The essence of repentance is a change of heart. To *repent* means to change your whole way of thinking. It is turning from sin and moving back toward God. Regardless of our sin, God isn't done with us. Listen to God's Word:

> *This is the word that came to Jeremiah from the Lord. Go down to the potter's house and there I will give you my message. So I went down to the potter's house and I saw him working at the wheel. But the pot he was shaping from the clay was marred in his hands; so the potter formed it into another pot, shaping it as seemed best to him.*
>
> *Then the word of the Lord came to me: "O house of Israel, can I not do with you as this potter does?" declares the Lord. "Like clay in the hand of the potter, so are you in my hand, O house of Israel"* (Jeremiah 18:1-6).

Perhaps you feel like *marred clay*. Perhaps you have been living a disobedient lifestyle. The good news is that God, who is the potter, has plans to form you into *another pot*. The Lord is not done with you. It's time to return to God.

What is Repentance?

Here is a summary of what repentance involves:

- Assuming full responsibility for your sin and blaming no one else.
- Refusing to compare your sins with the sins of others.
- An open, unguarded admission of everything you have kept a secret.
- A spirit that simply begs for mercy; claiming no rights and making no excuses.
- A desire to make a total and complete break with sin no matter the cost.
- A broken and humble spirit before God – not angry or proud.
- A willing and teachable spirit that is ready to obey God.
- Giving God the credit for turning your life around.

God does not expect you to become perfect, but He does want to see a visible change in your behavior and life direction. God sees your heart. He knows if you are being honest with Him. Whatever is denied cannot be healed. It's time to come clean. Walk away from the world of darkness and walk toward the kingdom of light.

Personal Restoration

Because sin is lethal, the sooner it is exposed the better. God has the power to break self-destructive habits and replace them with God-honoring choices that lead to personal restoration. God wants to replace your failure with a *fresh start*. God's pathway to personal restoration involves receiving love, learning truth and not giving up. This will require a teachable spirit – a willingness to trust God and learn from past mistakes. Four areas require our attention:

God

The foundation for our personal relationship with God is our time alone with Him. This includes Scripture reading, prayer, journal writing, spiritual reading, fellowship and counseling. These are vital disciplines. God will show us that a relationship with Him can provide more satisfaction than anything this world has to offer.

Spouse

Devastating sins destroy trust. Rebuilding trust takes time. It involves honest communication accompanied by consistent behavior. Both parties must reflect the grace of God by giving their spouse another chance. An unmarried person must find an accountability partner (of the same sex) to help him or her process God's truth and grace. The key is to find someone who is not afraid to be open, honest and direct. Accountable relationships protect us. As they say in Alcoholics Anonymous: *You're only as sick as your secrets.*

Friends

Family members will often support a fallen person because they are "family." Frankly, friends don't feel the same obligation. Many people do not know what to do when someone they trust lets them down. They feel confused, angry, disappointed and betrayed. The anger probably represents a stage of grief. You must give a friend time to process what's happened. Give him the same amount of understanding that you want him to give you.

If friends desert you, it is one of the consequences of your sin. Don't hold it against them. You may have done the same thing if the tables were turned. If you have friends that support you, don't minimize the need to rebuild their trust. Just because they can forgive does not mean they trust you. Thank God for the friends you have and if necessary, ask Him to give you new ones. God sometimes removes our relational network to teach us dependence.

Career

Sometimes personal failure is directly tied to a specific job or career field. Separation from an environment that leaves you vulnerable is essential. It may be wise to change your occupational role in order to give undivided attention to repentance.

To God, your testimony is more important than your title. Be open to God's career field and His job choice. Let go of your professional dreams and trust God with your occupational future.

From Glance To Gaze

In the book, *The Most Important Year in a Woman's Life / The Most Important Year in a Man's Life*, Robert Wolgemuth writes,

> Twenty years ago I worked on the second floor of a new office building. My desk faced the front window overlooking the parking lot. Early one day, I looked up from my desk in time to see a woman walking from her car into the building.
>
> She looked like a model. Her face and her body were flawless. Her stride was silky and strong. My heart raced as I watched until she disappeared into the building directly under my window.
>
> Wow, I thought to myself, I wonder who that is! The next morning, quite by accident, something caught my eye again. I looked up and saw the same woman walking from her car. My eyes didn't leave her until she was out of sight once more. For the next few mornings, the woman's appearance was no longer a surprise. I watched and waited for her. I stood at the window to get a better look.
>
> During the day, my mind would drift back to her. I began to think about how I might meet her – perhaps wait for her and act as though I was leaving the building as she approached.
>
> I had allowed my mind to go too far. I crossed the line and I knew it. "I've got to tell you something," I said to my wife Bobbie the next weekend. "There's a woman I see walking into the building every day..." For the next several minutes, I explained what had happened and how this mystery woman had captured my imagination.

> The burden of keeping a secret from Bobbie had become more than I wanted to carry. I told her that I was sorry and needed her forgiveness for my foolishness.
>
> She thanked me for telling her and willingly forgave me. Although I noticed the woman on Monday morning, my eyes left her before she made it to the front door. Because I had told Bobbie, the thrill of watching had evaporated.

Telling just one person about a specific temptation can diminish its power. Unrevealed secrets can hold you hostage. Confession allows others to assist you. When temptation comes, we all need protection. Everyone is vulnerable.

Would You Come and Get Me?

A man once told me how much he enjoyed walking along a beautiful coastline near his home that overlooked the ocean. On this particular coastline there was a lighthouse that stood on a volcanic rock that dropped off dramatically into the ocean. A curve in the highway allowed him to look across a bay and see a perfectly framed picture consisting of ocean, waves, lighthouse and cliffs.

His young daughter would often go with him. She was too small to see the lighthouse unless he lifted her up to look over a three-foot wall. She loved to walk on top of the wall, holding tightly to her father's hand. On the other side of the wall, the ground fell off at a very steep angle for several feet and then plunged straight down over the cliff to the ocean rocks hundreds of feet below.

Once, while his daughter was walking on top of the wall she turned to her father and said, "Daddy, if I ever fell over this wall would you come and get me?" Even though her father had a tremendous fear of heights, he reassured her. "Yes dear, I would come after you."

Someday, a person you know is going to fall away from the Lord and go *over the wall.* Jesus will ask you to go after him. Initially, how he or she got there won't matter. They are hurting and hoping that help is on the way.

Let the Lord use you despite your fears. He will tie a rope around your waist and lower you over the edge. Jesus wants you to go after the one who went over the wall.

Individual Response Questions

1. What encourages you most about the failures of famous Bible personalities?

2. When do you find yourself most vulnerable to temptation and personal failure?

3. What signs of *self-destruction* can you see more easily in others than yourself?

4. What aspect of repentance do you often overlook?

5. How can you use this lesson to help others?

6. What part of this lesson was most meaningful to you?

Personal Assessment

On a scale from 1-6, circle your response (1 means *not true* of you; 6 means *is true* of you).

- I consciously avoid situations that leave me vulnerable to temptation.

  1 2 3 4 5 6

- I make myself accountable to a mature believer in the area of my greatest weakness.

  1 2 3 4 5 6

- I am currently reaching out to a broken person.

  1 2 3 4 5 6

- I do not keep secrets from my spouse.

  1 2 3 4 5 6

- I believe that despite my sin, God can still use my life.

  1 2 3 4 5 6

Lesson 12 – Advancing the Kingdom

§

A Misunderstood Life

Ann Judson was the wife of Adoniram Judson, the famous missionary to Burma from 1812-1850. She was the first American woman missionary.

At age eighteen, Ann felt that God wanted her to be a missionary. What she didn't know was that God would send her to Burma. Her friends told her she was crazy and tried to discourage her. Her response was compelling. "If I could be the means of converting a single soul it would be worth spending my whole life to accomplish. I am not only willing to spend my days among the Burmese – I look forward to it."

Mr. Judson never promised her that it would be easy. Ann faced many difficult times. It took the Judson's four months by boat just to get to Burma. After six months, Ann got sick and had to leave to get medical help. Three years later, their first-born son mysteriously died at the age of eight months. In their ministry, seven years passed before the Judsons baptized their first convert.

In 1824, a war between England and Burma was declared. Mr. Judson and other missionaries were thrown into a Burmese prison and spent twenty months in a room with no ventilation. Each day, Ann brought him food and kept his hopes alive.

Following the war, the Judsons returned to their mission station. The mission house was now in ruin and all of their disciples had fled. Shortly thereafter, Ann came down with spotted fever and never recovered. In October 1826, she died at the age of thirty-seven.

Some may privately wonder if Ann Judson wasted her life. Many don't understand why a young, intelligent woman would give herself to a life of hardships. The notion that Ann was simply completing the work God had given her to do, didn't make sense.

What motivates a person to make such sacrifices? There are multiple answers: Ann believed it was a privilege to be God's messenger to Burma. In responding to God's call, she chose to live out her life on earth according to His will, not her own. She recognized that her life belonged to another. She simply accepted God's assignment for her life. In general, Ann Judson was motivated by three spiritual realities: God's Kingdom – God's Mission – God's Church.

God's Kingdom

The Scriptures speak of two entirely different realms – the *natural world* and the *kingdom of God*. These two realms are diametrically opposed to each other because they are dominated respectively by two separate wills – the will of fallen man, and the will of God.

In the **natural world,** fallen man is king. His will decides everything. Fallen man chooses who, what, when, where and why. He has boundless confidence in his own ability and an insatiable appetite for his own recognition.

He determines what's important – what is valued and what is rejected. He believes in his right to choose his own future. He never thinks twice about his right to dream his own dreams, set his own goals and make his own plans. When it comes to his life, he feels no obligation to ask anyone for permission – he knows what is best.

Fallen man may acknowledge God's existence, but he treats Him like a royal visitor from another country. God is permitted to decide nothing because He is merely a dignified guest, not Lord. Fallen man never wants to offend God, but nevertheless subtly reminds the Lord that this is his world. He will honor God with his lips but wants no interference. He will run his own life.

By contrast, in the **spiritual world,** God is the king. The kingdom of God is a realm where God decides everything without man's help. The kingdom of God is where God rules. Everything is done according to God's plan and timing. God chooses who, what, when, where and why. The kingdom of God consists of the spiritually poor – those who acknowledge that they have no power to save themselves. The self-sufficient are sent away; the destitute are welcomed.

God is our king and we are His representatives. Followers of Jesus don't choose God's mission – God chooses them for His missional purpose. Jesus said, *You did not choose Me, but I chose you, and appointed you, that you should go and bear fruit* (John 15:16).

John the Baptist said, *A man can only receive what is given to him from heaven* (John 3:27). Some people make their own plans and then ask God to bless them. Their motives may be sincere, but God's kingdom doesn't work that way. In God's kingdom, God initiates His own agenda, on His own terms, with His own timetable.

It wasn't Noah's idea to build an ark.

It wasn't Joseph's idea to move to Egypt.

It wasn't Mary's idea to have a son and name him Jesus.

In the Bible, there is no record of a God-fearing person who chose the life he wanted and then informed God of his decision. God's ways are not man's ways. The Scriptures teach us several important truths about the kingdom of God:

- THE KINGDOM OF GOD IS HERE NOW
  Jesus said, *The time has come. The kingdom of God is near. Repent and believe the good news* (Mark 1:15). There are times in life when we become acutely aware of God's presence. In these special moments, God makes His will known. God speaks directly to our hearts and we quickly discover the changes we must make.

  Whenever we pray, *Our Father in heaven, hallowed be your name, your kingdom come, your will be done on earth as it is in heaven* (Matthew 6:10), we are inviting God to make a fresh breakthrough into our world today.

- THE KINGDOM OF GOD IS WITHIN YOU
  Jesus was once asked about the physical nature of God's kingdom. He replied, *The kingdom of God does not come visibly, nor will people say, 'Here it is' or 'there it is,' because the kingdom of God is within you* (Luke 17:20-21).

  The rule and reign of God's kingdom begins in the human heart. It involves having a personal encounter with the Holy Spirit. Jesus said, *Unless a man is born again, he cannot see the kingdom of God* (John 3:3).

- THE KINGDOM OF GOD IS JESUS' TOP PRIORITY

  When people wanted to keep Jesus to themselves, Jesus replied, *I must preach the good news of the kingdom of God to the other towns also, because that is why I was sent* (Luke 4:43).

  Following His resurrection, Jesus focused on expanding His kingdom throughout the world. *He appeared to them over a period of forty days and spoke to them about the kingdom of God. You will be my witnesses in Jerusalem, and in all Judea and Samaria, and to the ends of the earth* (Acts 1:3, 8).

- THE KINGDOM OF GOD IS OUR FIRST CONCERN

  In Matthew 6:33, Jesus said, *But seek first his kingdom and his righteousness, and all these things will be given to you as well* (Matthew 6:33). God's people are instructed to not worry about the basic necessities of life such as food and clothing. God promises to provide. Followers of Jesus care more about the kingdom of God than anything else.

- THE KINGDOM OF GOD IS WORLDWIDE

  There is no geographic or national boundary to God's kingdom. He doesn't require a passport. The eyes of the Lord are everywhere and He always finds those who seek Him.

  From one man God made every nation of men that they should inhabit the whole earth; and he determined the times set for them and the exact places where they should live. God did this so that men would seek him and perhaps reach out for him and find him, though he is not far from each one of us (Acts 17:26-27).

- THE KINGDOM OF GOD IS ETERNAL

  The indestructible kingdom of God is a central theme in Scripture. David wrote, *The Lord has established his throne in heaven, and his kingdom rules over all* (Psalm 103:19).

  The kings of ancient Babylon declared this reality. *His kingdom is an eternal kingdom; his dominion endures from generation to generation. His kingdom will not be destroyed and his dominion will never end* (Daniel 4:3; 6:26).

  An angel told Mary, *He will be great and will be called the Son of the Most High; his kingdom will never end* (Luke 1:32-33). God's kingdom is as vast as God himself.

God's Mission

Followers of Jesus are His representatives. The Bible reveals that people are created for a special purpose. Foundationally, individuals are created to reflect the image of God. In His image, the Body of Christ (the Church) exists to carry out God's mission in the same way that Christ was sent to accomplish the Father's purpose. Ultimately, followers of Jesus exist to bring God glory.

Every follower of Jesus is *sent*. Followers of Jesus exist to make Christ's invisible kingdom visible and to complete God's mission on earth. Every believer in Jesus Christ is commissioned as His disciple to *go and minister* His life and love. There is a distinct assignment for each of us. As God's mission involved sending Jesus, Christ's mission involves sending you. Our Lord's numerous references to *being sent* did not go unnoticed by the apostle John.

John 5:30	I do not seek my own will, but the will of Him who *sent* me.
John 6:38	For I have come down from heaven not to do my own will, but the will of Him who *sent* me,
John 7:29	I know Him; because I am from Him and He *sent* me.
John 8:29	And He who *sent* me is with me; He has not left me alone, for I always do the things that are pleasing to Him.
John 12:44-45	He who believes in me does not believe in me, but in Him who *sent* me. And he who beholds me beholds the one who *sent* me.
John 13:20	He who receives whomever I *send* receives me; and he who receives me receives Him who *sent* me.
John 20:21	As the Father has *sent* me, I am *sending* you.

The impetus for mission resides in Christ who invites His followers to become His missional body on earth. He sends us to represent Him. God wants us to give a personal testimony of the difference Jesus has made in our life. He does not want you to be intimidated. Jesus is supporting you with all the resources that the Father provided Him.

God's Church

Followers of Christ are a *counterculture,* not a *subculture.* The Church is God's people, led by God's Spirit, to accomplish God's mission. It is a reproducing community of authentic disciples, being equipped and sent by God, to live and proclaim His kingdom in their world. The Church of Jesus Christ exists to present living proof of a loving God to a watching world.

The true Church is a spiritual phenomenon that has no human explanation. Christ's Church is a multi-racial, multi-cultural community. They come from every tribe, language, and nation on earth. They dwell on earth but their citizenship is in heaven. They promote the cause of a rejected and crucified man who claimed to be God. They believe the promise of His second coming.

In the meantime, they carry His cross, act as His representatives and do well to all men in His name. Every deed begins with God's will and ends with God's glory. They are willing to be misunderstood for the sake of Christ. They have no hard feelings toward anyone – only the desire to share the gospel of God's grace so that all men may repent and have peace with God.

The Church exists because God is on a mission. God's mission is directed toward all people. He loves all ethnic groups. He has no favorite nation, location or denomination. Every member of Christ's body is a participant in God's mission. This means leaving our place of security and going to where others are. Sometimes that means across the street. Other times that means across the ocean. In his book, *An Unstoppable Force,* Erwin Raphael McManus writes,

> The life of the Church is the heart of God. The heart of God is to serve a broken world. The Church cannot live when the heart of God is not beating within her. God's heartbeat is to seek and save that which is lost. The Church exists to serve as the body of Christ, and it is through this commitment to serve that we are forced to engage the culture.
>
> The serving that we are required to do requires direct contact. You cannot wash the feet of a dirty world if you refuse to touch it. There is a sense of mystery to this, but it is in serving that the Church finds her strength. When she ceases to serve the world around her, she begins to atrophy. In pathology, atrophy is the wasting or decreasing in size of any part of the body.
>
> When the Church refuses to serve the world, she begins to waste away. She finds herself deteriorating, withering and losing her strength.

The Church is not a building, but an assembly of individuals. The Church is what the members are – no better and no worse. If individual members within a local church are growing and serving – then that's what the church is. If individual members are stagnant and indifferent – then that's what the church is. God wants a Church that is ablaze for Him. He wants us to build bridges for His kingdom in business, education and government. His aim is far beyond church programs held on church property. He sends us to transform neighborhoods, cities and nations.

Spiritual Practices

As His representative, Ann Judson lived to advance God's kingdom and accomplish God's mission. How did she do it? How does anyone do it? How do we keep our vision clear and our passion hot year after year? The desire to give up, quit or at least slow down is real.

What are the priorities that followers of Jesus need to develop so that their lives are a fresh and fragrant aroma to the world around them? From Scripture, here are two spiritual practices.

Self-Feeding

The first practice is the commitment to be a self-feeding disciple. A growing disciple of Jesus takes responsibility for the feeding, fueling and filling of his own heart. Jesus modeled the importance of spending time alone with the Father. *Very early in the morning, while it was still dark, Jesus got up, left the house and went off to a solitary place, where he prayed* (Mark 1:35).

As His disciples, we too are dependent. We know that fire tends to go out. The people in the Bible who we respect took responsibility for their own time alone with God.

Moses — *Now Moses used to take a tent and pitch it outside the camp some distance away, calling it the "tent of meeting"…the Lord spoke with Moses…the Lord would speak to Moses face to face, as a man speaks with a friend* (Exodus 33:7, 11).

Joshua — *Moses would return to the camp, but Joshua did not leave the tent* (Exodus 33:11).

Samuel — *The Lord was with Samuel as he grew up, and he let none of his words fall to the ground. The Lord continued to appear at Shiloh, and there he revealed himself to Samuel through his word* (I Samuel 3:19, 21).

DAVID — *Blessed is the man who does not walk in the counsel of the wicked or stand in the way of sinners or sit in the seat of scoffers. But his delight is in the law of the Lord, and on his law he meditates day and night* (Psalm 1:1-2).

DANIEL — *Three times a day he got down on his knees and prayed, giving thanks to his God just as he had done before* (Daniel 6:10).

APOSTLES — *Brothers, choose seven men from among you who are known to be full of the Spirit and wisdom. We will turn this responsibility over to them and will give our attention to prayer and the ministry of the word* (Acts 6:3-4).

These people took responsibility for tending the fire on the altar of their hearts. In his book, *Power through Prayer,* E. M. Bounds writes,

> The church is looking for better methods; God is looking for better men. What the church needs today is not more or better machinery, not new organizations or more and novel methods. She needs men – men mighty in prayer.
>
> The Holy Spirit does not flow through methods, but through men. He does not come upon machinery, but on men. He does not anoint plans, but men of prayer.

Without spiritual nourishment, a disciple will not grow. In his book, *The Ragamuffin Gospel,* Brennan Manning writes, "Spiritual reading is, or at least can be, second only to prayer as a developer and support of the inner life."

When the pace of life is high-speed, people become drained of the energy they need to be self-feeding disciples. In his book, *Restoring Your Spiritual Passion,* Gordon MacDonald tells a story from African colonial history:

> In the deep jungles of Africa, a traveler was making a long journey. Natives had been engaged from tribe to tribe to carry the loads. The first day they marched rapidly and went far. The traveler had high hopes of a speedy journey.
>
> But the second morning these jungle tribesmen refused to move. On inquiry as to the reason for this strange behavior, the traveler was informed that they had gone too fast the first day and they were now waiting for their souls to catch up with their bodies.

If we never develop the skill of self-feeding, we will be continually malnourished. We all benefit from good teaching, but we must not depend upon others alone for our spiritual nourishment. Jesus *died* for us, but will not *read* for us. We must learn to feed ourselves.

Ministry Partners

The second spiritual practice is the commitment to develop ministry partners. Discipleship is a team sport. We cannot complete God's mission alone. While on earth, Jesus devoted much of His time to training the trainers. With the entire world to save, He called twelve men to be *with Him*.

Equipping involves training. Jesus created an *equipping group,* not a *support group*. He trained the apostles to follow Him and fish for men. He also trained them to work together. His disciples began as learning partners and finished as ministry partners. In Scripture, we find many examples of ministry partners. In the book of Romans, the apostle Paul identifies twenty-six ministry partners (ten of which are women). Other examples include:

Moses and Aaron	Exodus 5:1
Moses and Joshua	Numbers 11:28; Exodus 32:11
Joshua and Caleb	Numbers 14:6
David and Jonathan	I Samuel 20:17
Elijah and Elisha	II Kings 2:9
Disciples sent two by two	Luke 10:1
Peter and John	Acts 3:1
Paul and Barnabas	Acts 13:2
Barnabas and John Mark	Acts 15:39
Paul and Silas	Acts 15:40
Paul and Timothy	Acts 16:1-3; Philippians 2:22
Paul and Titus	II Corinthians 8:23

Because discouragement is such a front line issue, we all need ministry partners. Ministry partners are individual teammates. They sponsor us, work with us, encourage, rebuke, and pray for us. They form a deeper relationship than mere Christian friends. A ministry partner can lift your spirit with just the sound of his voice.

In 1990, General Norman Schwarzkopf was Commander in Chief of U.S. Forces in Operation Desert Shield, undertaken to prevent Iraq from moving against Saudi Arabia. During the days of the war, he assembled 765,000 troops from twenty-eight countries, hundreds of ships and thousands of planes and tanks. General Schwarzkopf called General Colin Powell, then Chairman of the Joint Chiefs of Staff, every evening on the telephone to discuss the events of the day.

One day a news reporter asked, "Why?" Schwartzkopf answered, "He is the only person in the world who knows what I am trying to do. He listens to my ideas, helps me form strategies, and exposes my errors in judgment – *daily*." Now that's a ministry partner!

Die to Live

Millard Fuller is the founder of *Habitat for Humanity,* a non-profit Christian housing ministry that builds homes for the homeless. When he entered the University of Alabama Law School in 1957, he and a friend invested their money in real estate. By graduation, they were clearing $50,000 annually. They launched a mail order business and by 1964, employed 150 people. By age twenty-nine, Millard Fuller was almost a millionaire.

At this juncture, his life began to fall apart. He was a workaholic and his wife asked him to cut back. He promised to reduce his hours but never did. Finally, she left him. Alone in a New York hotel room, he realized that he had traded his wife and family for his career. Millard Fuller was a millionaire who had everything money could buy – but was not happy. His definition of success had been reduced to more money, more buildings, and more things.

After coming to himself, Millard Fuller was ready to die to the dream of **being a success** and live to the dream of **being a blessing.** He turned to God and reconciled with his wife. He sold all of his assets and along with his wife Linda, started *Habitat for Humanity.*

By 1972, twenty-seven homes were built. Today, *Habitat for Humanity International* operates in all 50 states in the United States and in dozens of other countries. They have built over 400,000 homes and have served more than 2 million people around the world. "You get a real sense of joy in this work," says Millard after a long day on a roof. "The most dynamic people I know are concerned about something beyond themselves. We're doing something that makes a real difference. It won't fade away next week or next month."

Millard Fuller discovered treasures the world cannot see. It happens every time someone makes the kingdom of God his top priority. Perhaps it is time for you to come to yourself. God is inviting you to die to the dream of being a success and live to the dream of being a blessing.

Individual Response Questions

1. What is the difference between the natural world and kingdom of God?

2. Which characteristic of the kingdom of God is most significant to you?

3. Does the idea of Jesus *sending you* inspire or intimidate you? Why?

4. How can you learn to become a self-feeding disciple?

5. How do you develop ministry partners? Where do you begin?

6. What part of this lesson was most meaningful to you?

Personal Assessment

On a scale from 1-6, circle your response (1 means *not true* of you; 6 means *is true* of you).

- My commitment to God's kingdom, mission and church is getting stronger.

  1 2 3 4 5 6

- I am living to the dream of being a blessing.

  1 2 3 4 5 6

- I am engaging my friends, neighbors and work associates in the places God has put me.

  1 2 3 4 5 6

- I am developing self-feeding habits. I do not get all of my spiritual nourishment from others.

  1 2 3 4 5 6

- My ministry partner encourages and challenges me.

  1 2 3 4 5 6

Lesson 13 – The Story of Your Life

§

The Leading Character

In the fall of 2000, our daughter Crystal was a junior at Asbury College. She called home one evening and said, "Dad, I have been seeking God's direction for my life. Following graduation, I want to teach music in China."

This was the first time I remember Crystal mentioning the idea of China. At first, I didn't know what to say. So, with a cautious tone, I said, "That sounds good. Let's keep praying and I'm sure God will make it clear to both of us."

After we hung up, I began to mull this over. Carey had been to Africa twice. Now, Crystal is talking about China. I hadn't even been to North Dakota.

Seriously, what bothered me most is that I never imagined our daughters living on one side of the world, while Peggy and I lived on the other. Then, God spoke to my heart. "Paul, I am in the business of guiding people. It's my specialty." I knew the Lord was right, but there is nothing natural about letting someone else choose the direction of your life.

During the next two years, God began to prepare Peggy and me for the reality that our daughter might someday live in China. A breakthrough came when we were asked to start a Bible study with a group of Chinese scholars at Creighton University. It was through this experience that God convinced me that He knew what He was doing.

In 2002, Crystal received an offer to be the music teacher of the Shenyang International School in Shenyang, China. Shortly before her departure, a man came to our Chinese Bible study. He was the husband of one of our regular members, but had never attended because he lived in another city. At the end of the study, the man approached me. I'll never forget what he said.

"I hear that your daughter will soon be living in Shenyang. That is my hometown. I know many people there. Here is my business card. If she has a problem, just let me know. I will contact my friends and someone will take care of it. You have my word."

That encounter caused me to look at two verses in a new light. *I know, O Lord, that a man's life is not his own; it is not for man to determine his steps* (Jeremiah 10:23). *All the days ordained for me were written in your book before one of them came to be* (Psalm 139:16). These and other scriptures reveal an amazing truth: **God is the leading character in the story of our life.**

The Power Behind Your Story

In the Bible, there is only one miracle that is recorded four separate times. It is the miracle of Jesus feeding *five thousand men, besides women and children* (Matthew 14:21). He fed them through the faith of one young boy. Ironically, we do not know any personal facts about this boy. We don't know his name, age, where he lived, or anything about his family.

The only thing we know is that over five thousand people ran out of food – everyone but one boy. *The Message* paraphrase describes the story this way:

> *When Jesus looked out and saw that a large crowd had arrived, he said to Philip, "Where can we buy bread to feed these people?" He said this to stretch Philip's faith. He already knew what he was going to do. Philip answered, "Two hundred silver pieces wouldn't be enough to buy bread for each person to get a piece."*
>
> *One of the disciples – Andrew, brother to Simon Peter – said, "There's a little boy here who has five barley loaves and two fish. But that's a drop in the bucket for a crowd like this." Jesus said, "Make the people sit down." There was a nice carpet of green grass in this place. They sat down, about five thousand of them.*
>
> *Then Jesus took the bread and, having given thanks, gave it to those who were seated. He did the same with the fish. All five thousand ate as much as they wanted* (John 6:5-11).

I am confident that this day turned out much differently than the little boy anticipated. Even though he trusted Jesus, he never dreamed that such a small amount of food could feed so many. The power behind this story is not in the little boy or his lunch. The power is in Jesus – the One to whom he gave his lunch.

On that day, Jesus already knew what He was going to do. Eventually, everyone learned what the Lord had in mind. In his book, *Eat This Book,* Eugene Peterson writes,

> None of us is the leading character in the story of our life. When we submit our lives to what we read in Scripture, we find that we are not being led to see God in our stories but our stories in God's. God is the larger context and plot in which our stories find themselves.

Recognizing God's Hand

Once we realize that none of us is the leading character in the story of our life, we begin to notice God's providential leading. It is God's intervention in our lives that reminds us that *He* is the leading character. The things that happen in your life are things God allows for a reason. God doesn't make mistakes. In his book, *We Travel an Appointed Way,* A. W. Tozer writes,

> To the child of God, there is no such thing as an accident. He travels an appointed way...Accidents may indeed appear to befall him and misfortune stalk his way; but these evils will be so in appearance only and will seem evil only because we cannot read the secret script of God's hidden providence.

Over the centuries, godly men and women have reflected on the mystery of God's providence. In their moment of need, they discovered this principle: *When you cannot see God's hand, trust God's heart*. You will find five recurring statements of faith in their writings:

- God is always reliable, but never predictable.
- God brought me to this place. This is God's appointment.
- God will give me the grace to behave as His child. His love is sufficient.
- God is refining me. In the end, this trial will turn into a blessing.
- God will bring me out in His time. He alone knows when and how.

God has a plan and He is behind everything that is happening in our lives – from birth to death. His hand writes many chapters in the story of our lives. He turns us around, grants us another chance, helps us face opposition, and gives us hope. As you read the following true-life episodes, see if you can recognize elements of your own life story.

Turn You Around

I once sold a life insurance policy to a young man named Jerry (not his real name). I told Jerry that to qualify for the policy there would be a blood test. He said, "No problem." Three weeks later he was "approved."

When I walked into his office to deliver the contract he nervously said, "Come in and shut the door." With a totally serious face he continued, "I have prayed more in the last three weeks than I have my entire life."

"For the last three weeks, I have been reflecting on my life. I didn't sleep at all the night before the nurse came to draw my blood. When she told me to roll up my sleeve and hold out my arm, my whole life flashed in front of my eyes. I remembered all the stupid choices I made and the reckless lifestyle I lived."

"When the nurse put the needle into my arm I knew God was telling me, 'the party is over.' It was my moment of truth – you know, like judgment day! Not only does God know, but now everyone will find out – my family, friends and work associates – everyone!"

"Jerry, find out what?" I asked.

"If I am HIV positive!" he said. "I was so scared because I didn't know what was going to happen next. But when you called and told me that I was approved with no problems, I knew God had given me a break. I knew that God didn't hate me. I knew there was hope."

There is no limit to the different ways God can get our attention. God was not mad at Jerry – He was trying to turn him around. God is not mad at you, either. God is not trying to pay you back – He's trying to turn you around.

He simply wants you to recognize that none of us is the leading character in the story of our life.

Second Chance

In his book, *Fresh Power,* Pastor Jim Cymbala tells the story of David Berkowitz, the infamous *Son of Sam* from the New York City murders in 1977. In 1953, Berkowitz was adopted by practicing Jewish parents. He knew virtually nothing about Jesus.

As a young adult, his crimes began as random acts of violence. He tossed big rocks off overpasses into traffic. He started setting fires of all kinds – two thousand in all, which he logged in a journal. Then, Berkowitz got involved in a satanic cult. He prayed to demons to guide his murders.

After his arrest, he pleaded guilty to killing five women and one man as well as wounding many others. He was sentenced to over 300 years in prison. In 1979 an inmate slit his throat. The doctors in the prison couldn't understand how he lived. Eight years later he was moved to the Sullivan Correctional Facility.

There, an inmate named Ricky Lopez approached him and said, "David, Jesus loves you and has a purpose for your life." Berkowitz laughed and said, "You don't know who you are talking to. No one could love someone who had committed such horrible crimes."

Ricky talked to him every day and gave him a small New Testament with Psalms. Since David was Jewish, he suggested that he start with the Psalms. His turning point was Psalm 118:5: *In my anguish I cried to the Lord; and He answered by setting me free.*

Soon after, he knelt by his bunk and asked Jesus Christ to be his Savior. Today, Berkowitz is not only a follower of Jesus – he is the Chaplain's Assistant at the Sullivan Correctional Facility. Cymbala writes,

> David has now spent half his life behind bars. He will never be paroled. In fact, he has never asked me or any other minister or organization to plead for his release.
>
> He knows his crimes were so serious that he deserves to be locked up for life and he says the prison is his God-ordained sphere of ministry. To leave this setting, he says, would be to run from the call of God on his life, the way Jonah did. There's plenty to do here.

David Berkowitz didn't get a *get out of jail free card* – he got a purpose for living. God didn't give him a pardon from prison – He gave him a ministry in prison. David Berkowitz recognized that second chances are always available when repentance is real.

A sinful past does not prevent a promising future when God is the leading character of your life.

Courage

The people in the Bible we admire most possessed the courage to face opposition. They dared to take a stand. They chose God over family and friends and kept going when others turned back. Sooner or later, everyone faces opposition.

Jesus was ridiculed and thrown out of His own hometown. On one occasion He ignored His own mother and brothers when they thought He was out of His mind (Mark 3:21; 31-35). Often, the most negative response will come from the people we least suspect.

When A.B. Simpson became the pastor of the 13th Street Presbyterian Church in New York City, he asked for permission to bring into the church approximately one hundred Italian converts which he had won while preaching on the streets of poor neighborhoods.

Unfortunately, his fellow church leaders told him that the Italians needed to find their own fellowship. They weren't socially equal with the rest of the members of the church. Simpson graciously accepted their decision and turned in his resignation. He then started *The Christian and Missionary Alliance*. It takes real courage to ignore the response of others.

In his book, *The Cry and the Covenant,* Morton Thompson describes the incredible true story of Dr. Ignaz Philipp Semmelweis. Although he was one of history's greatest doctors, this man was persecuted by his colleagues and is virtually forgotten by the world.

Dr. Semmelweis lived when a savage epidemic of childbed fever swept across Europe in the 1840's. In those days, one out of six women died in childbirth simply because doctors would perform autopsies and then turn right around and make pelvic examinations on expectant mothers without ever pausing to wash their hands. Dr. Semmelweis understood what was happening. He instituted the practice of washing in a chlorine solution before examining his patients.

Dr. Semmelweis lived by an oath that he shared with the midwives of his day. "I swear by the Almighty and the all-knowing God that I shall never mistreat patients entrusted to my care."

In eleven years, he delivered 8,537 babies with the loss of only 184 mothers. As a result, he lost his job. He moved from city to city but was rejected by older and more experienced physicians. In one of his most famous lectures to a medical society in 1848 he said,

> Doctors, I have shown that this dreaded fever is caused by decomposed material coming in contact with a patient. This infection can arise after surgery, as well as after childbirth. I have shown how it can be prevented. I have proved all that I have said with facts, records, experiments, and with human beings. I have talked a great deal.
>
> But while we talk, gentlemen, women are dying and doctors are killing them. They are dying from childbed fever in all of our hospitals. We talk, gentlemen. We talk and talk and talk. I'm not asking for anything world shaking. I am only asking you to wash.
>
> In the name of pity, stop murdering these mothers. Wash your hands, gentlemen. Wash everything that contacts the patient. For God's sake, wash your hands.

Over time, Semmelweis became totally dejected. He was losing his mind. He overheard family members talking about putting him away in an asylum. Realizing that time was running out, he printed a large bundle of flyers. He ran frantically through the streets, giving them to every young man and woman he passed. In bold letters, the leaflet read:

> Young men and women! You are in mortal danger! The peril of childbed fever menaces your life! Beware of doctors, for they will kill you! Remember! When you enter labor, unless everything that touches you is washed with soap, water, and then chlorine solution, you will die and your child with you!
>
> I can no longer appeal to the doctors! I appeal to you! Protect yourselves! Your friend, Ignaz Philipp Semmelweis.

When all the circulars were distributed, there was one last thing. Dr. Semmelweis ran into a local clinic and burst into the dissection room. To prove once-and-for-all how decomposed material can infect an open wound, he seized a knife.

He slashed open the stomach of a dead woman. He then cut his fingers and plunged his hand into her contaminated body. He drew back his hand and sighed in relief. He was now free.

The next day his family took him to a mental hospital where he eventually died at age forty-seven. He died of the very disease that he devoted his life to eradicate. His washbasins were discarded and his colleagues were laughing in his face. The death-rattle of a thousand women was ringing in his ears.

Today we know he was right. Modern medicine owes Semmelweis a debt it can never repay. Why? He possessed the courage to ignore the response of others. None of us should be naïve. Faith requires courage. Just as Jesus paid a price to follow God's leading, we will pay a price to follow Christ's leading.

Hope

In 1966, John and Donna Bechtel were sent to Hong Kong as missionaries by *The Christian & Missionary Alliance*. They were assigned to work with young people. At that time, the population of Hong Kong was four million people and over two million were under age 18.

Bechtel soon learned from government officials that they were having trouble with their young people and they didn't know what to do. He told the officials, "I can help. I have a dream to build a youth camp – but I don't have any land. Would you be willing to donate some land?"

A government official said, "There's a 153 acre island called *Sunshine Island*. We can give it to you, but it needs a pier. If you can build a pier, it's yours – but that will cost you $40,000." Bechtel told his friends in America, "We have the opportunity of a lifetime. Pray and send money." But no money came in.

John returned to the government official and said, "Obviously, the island is not the right place. Would you please consider giving us a place on a beach somewhere?" The official said, "We have seven acres on a place called *Castle Peak Beach*. But before we give you the land you have to build a dormitory costing $40,000."

Bechtel began to realize that $40,000 was clearly the magic number and was getting discouraged. He got on his knees and prayed, "Lord, help us."

About that time, Anthony Bollback, the field chairman in Hong Kong telephoned John and said, "There's an organization that runs orphanages around the world. They have an orphanage in Hong Kong that is having financial difficulties." They approached the organization, told them of their dream and asked them if they would consider giving them the orphanage.

The head of the organization said, "We just a built a building on the property for over a million dollars – so we can't give it to you but we will sell it to you." Anthony and John doubled their prayers. The next day they received word. The board would sell the orphanage for $240,000.

By now, John felt hopeless. His dream of building a camp was almost dead.

Within days, Walter Meloon, an influential businessman came to Hong Kong, saw the orphanage and said, "John this is an opportunity of a lifetime. Don't worry about a thing. I'll go back to the U.S. and raise all the money you need." Three months later Mr. Meloon wrote a letter. It began, "Dear John, O how I hate to write you this letter. I was not able to raise any money for the camp."

John's heart sank, but he kept reading. "P.S. Enclosed, please find a letter from a 14-year-old girl named Belinda Holmes." Her letter read, "Dear Mr. Bechtel, Here is my ice cream money for two weeks. Please use this one dollar to buy the camp."

John Bechtel showed the letter to the head of the organization that owned the orphanage and said, "We have the money to buy the camp – read this letter." The man was so moved by the girl's letter that he sent it to his board in the United States. They voted to sell the property for $1.00.

Suen Douh Camp (Preach the Gospel Camp) was purchased for $1.00.

The camp covered 4.5 acres and included dormitories for 350 kids, an auditorium for 450 people, staff housing, an athletic field, basketball court, and a large supply of chopsticks, bowls and rice. It was ready for immediate occupation.

Since its inception in 1971, 1.2 million young people have attended and 116,000 have accepted Jesus as their Savior. Once, John was eating dinner at a Chinese restaurant in Paris, France. His server was from Hong Kong and told John about attending the camp. The server said, "I asked Jesus into my heart at that camp." John replied, "Well, I helped start it."

The server's eyes got as big as silver dollars and immediately brought another server to John's table. "We both asked Jesus into our hearts at *Suen Douh Camp*." All of this happened because one dollar of ice cream money was given to Jesus.

Just when we're ready to give up, God gives us hope. We must live with the assumption that God is doing more than we are aware of. Jesus always knows what He is going to do – whether He's working with one lunch, or one dollar. None of us is the leading character in the story of our life.

Individual Response Questions

1. What did Tozer mean when he wrote, "The children of God travel an appointed way?"

2. In the story of your life, when did God turn you around and give you another chance?

3. In the story of your life, when did you need courage to face negative responses from others?

4. In the story of your life, when did an unexpected blessing give you hope?

5. What does *none of us is the leading character in the story of our life* mean to you?

6. What part of this lesson was most meaningful to you?

Personal Assessment

On a scale from 1-6, circle your response (1 means *not true* of you; 6 means *is true* of you).

- I am confident that God is behind everything that is happening in my life.

  1 2 3 4 5 6

- My behavior reflects my belief that I am not the leading character in the story of my life.

  1 2 3 4 5 6

- Despite my past mistakes, I am allowing God to use my life.

  1 2 3 4 5 6

- I have the courage to ignore the response of others.

  1 2 3 4 5 6

- I am trusting Jesus to lead my life.

  1 2 3 4 5 6

Leader Guide

§

You will find this study easy to lead. Each lesson is clearly written. The real life stories will help you apply the scriptural principles. Here are some additional suggestions:

- What is the purpose of this study?

What's Missing Inside You? explains foundational principles for Christian living. Keep that in mind. Don't allow the discussion to veer off on tangents this study does not address.

- Where do I begin?

When you meet for the first time, make sure everyone has a copy of the book. While married couples may want to share one copy, it is not recommended. The questions and the assessment at the end of each lesson are personal.

Next, read aloud the *Intent of This Study* and *Getting the Most from This Study*. Take time to clarify the expectations. Finish your first session by reading aloud the *Spiritual Terms*. As you proceed, discuss these questions:

1. How does this description of the Bible compare with your current understanding? On a scale from 1-10, how familiar are you with the Bible?

2. What do "Father, Son and Holy Spirit" mean to you? Are these terms familiar?

3. Do you believe that Satan is real? Why?

4. How does the term "Christian" vary in meaning from culture to culture? Why is "follower of Jesus" clearer?

- ## How do I maximize each session?

1. Review the lesson summary and Bible people index

The *Lesson Summary* will assist you in emphasizing the main points of each lesson. Beyond emphasizing the main points, ask, "How does this apply to our lives today?" At the end of the study you will find a listing of the Bible people who are referenced.

2. Reinforce expectations

As you conclude each week, remind members to do their homework: Read the next lesson and make note of any concept that was significant. Write a brief answer to all of the individual response questions. Complete the personal assessment.

3. Resist the pressure to rush

Jesus taught people, not lessons. There is no perfect schedule for this study. You may require more than one session to work through each lesson.

4. Facilitate group discussion

It is not necessary to discuss every question or follow the order given. Be aware that someone may ask a question that the lesson does not address. Keep the discussion focused on the subject at hand. The discussion questions will stimulate sharing. The personal assessment will encourage honesty. Conclude each session by asking members to share what part of the lesson was most meaningful to them.

5. Encourage self-disclosure

The *Personal Assessment* is not intended to create guilt or comparisons. Everyone is in process. When we go to the doctor we are weighed. It isn't usually fun, but it does reveal reality. The *Personal Assessment* helps people "stand on the scale" and be real. At a minimum, ask members to share their score on two personal assessment statements. A simple approach is one-on-one sharing, men with men and women with women.

Lesson Summary

§

This study is about relationship and representation. It has two sections. Lessons 1-6 will develop your personal relationship with God. Lessons 7-13 explore the reason God made you and how to be His representative.

Throughout thirteen lessons, you will discover eight life-changing insights. Four are about God: He is our *Father, Savior, Guide* and *King*. Four are about us: We are His *Child, Temple, Disciple* and *Representative*.

Beginning with lesson 5, the material is addressed to believers. Lessons 6-13 will be instructive, yet challenging for those who have not trusted Christ for themselves.

Lesson 1	Main Idea:	**God Created Everything**
	Key Thoughts:	There is only one God. Man is created in God's image. Our view of God affects our view of others.
Lesson 2	Main Idea:	**Man is God's Dwelling Place**
	Key Thoughts:	God created man to reflect His likeness. Without God, people are spiritually dead. People often reflect what sin is like.
Lesson 3	Main Idea:	**Who Jesus Is**
	Key Thoughts:	Jesus came from heaven to die for us. Jesus is the good news of the gospel. By sending Jesus, God personally visited us.

Lesson 4	Main Idea:	**A Fresh Start**
	Key Thoughts:	Being born again is the same as being saved. Salvation is a personal miracle. Ask Jesus into your heart today.
Lesson 5	Main Idea:	**Spiritual Identity**
	Key Thoughts:	God is our Father. We are His children. Children of God are accepted, secure and content. Jesus frees us from worrying about what others think.
Lesson 6	Main Idea:	**Total Forgiveness**
	Key Thoughts:	Forgiveness is a difficult lesson to learn. We must forgive others as we have been forgiven. Forgiveness is a powerful testimony of God's love.
Lesson 7	Main Idea:	**The Holy Spirit**
	Key Thoughts:	The Holy Spirit is often neglected and forgotten. The Person of the Holy Spirit is just as real as Jesus. Followers of Jesus are the temple of the Holy Spirit.
Lesson 8	Main Idea:	**The Flesh and Self-life**
	Key Thoughts:	The flesh is man's natural instincts apart from God. The self-life is the root of our struggle to obey God. Only Jesus can change human nature.
Lesson 9	Main Idea:	**Becoming Like Jesus**
	Key Thoughts:	To be Christ-like we must offer ourselves to God. The Holy Spirit wants to fill every part of our lives. There is no formula for being filled with the Spirit.

Lesson 10	Main Idea:	**God's Power**
	Key Thoughts:	We must admit our need for spiritual power. God provides the power; we provide the means. As members of His body, Jesus works through us.
Lesson 11	Main Idea:	**Personal Failure**
	Key Thoughts:	Followers of Jesus are vulnerable to temptation. Self-destruction happens gradually. God offers strength and hope.
Lesson 12	Main Idea:	**God's Kingdom**
	Key Thoughts:	Followers of Jesus invest in the kingdom of God. The Father sent Jesus. Now, Jesus sends us. We are His representatives in the world.
Lesson 13	Main Idea:	**God's Guidance**
	Key Thoughts:	Jesus always knows what He's going to do. There is a reason for the things God allows. We can trust God to lead our life.

Bible People Index

§

Listed below, in alphabetical order, is a brief description of the Bible people who are referenced in *What's Missing Inside You?*

Abraham	The husband of Sarah and the father of Isaac, the name Abraham means the "father of many nations." He is the first of the three patriarchs (Genesis 17:5).
Adam	The first male created by God (Genesis 2:7).
Andrew	One of the twelve apostles, Andrew is the brother of Simon Peter (Matthew 4:18).
Cornelius	A Roman Centurion, Cornelius is the first prominent Gentile to be converted to Christianity (Acts 10:1).
Daniel	A young Jew known for his visions, Daniel and three friends, Hananiah, Mishael and Azariah, were taken captive by Nebuchadnezzar, king of Babylon. Daniel and his friends influenced the king. (Daniel 1:6).
David	The second king of Israel, David is most famous for killing the giant, Goliath, committing adultery with Bathsheba and writing many of the Psalms (II Samuel 16:12-13).
Eve	The first female created by God (Genesis 2:21-22; 3:20).
Isaac	Born to the hundred-year-old Abraham and the ninety-year-old Sarah, Isaac is the second of the three patriarchs (Genesis 21:5).

Isaiah	A prophet to the Jewish nation around 730 BC, Isaiah is the author of the longest prophetic book in the Old Testament.
Jacob	The son of Isaac and the grandson of Abraham, Jacob is the third of the three patriarchs. His son's names are those of the twelve tribes of Israel. God changed Jacob's name to Israel (Genesis 23:28).
James	One of the twelve apostles, James is the brother of John (Matthew 4:21).
Jesus	The central person of the Bible, Jesus is the Son of God who came from heaven. He lived a sinless life and was crucified on a cross. His death was a voluntary sacrifice for the sins of the world. After he was raised from the dead, Jesus ascended to heaven. Today, He is alive and seated at the right hand of God (Philippians 2:8-11; Hebrews 1:3).
John	One of the twelve apostles, John is the brother of James. He was a leader in the early church (Acts 3:1; 4:1). John wrote four New Testament books: the gospel of John, I, II, and III John, and the book of Revelation.
John the Baptist	John the "baptizer" prepared people for the coming of Jesus. He baptized Jesus and was beheaded by King Herod. (Matthew 3:13-15).
Jonah	Jonah is a prophet who was sent to warn the city of Nineveh. He fled from the Lord and was swallowed by a large fish. After repenting, God have him another chance. (Jonah 1:1-3; 3:1-3).
Joseph	Several people in the Bible bear the name *Joseph*. In the Old Testament, Joseph is the favorite son of Jacob. He was sold by his brothers as a slave, falsely accused and put in prison. In Egypt, God rescued Joseph and he became the Prime Ministry under Pharaoh. Joseph learned that God sent him to Egypt to save lives and preserve a nation (Genesis 45:5). In the New Testament, Joseph is the husband of Mary and earthly father of Jesus. Joseph intended to divorce Mary when he learned that she was pregnant. An angel intervened and revealed God's plan. Joseph was a carpenter. (Matthew 1:18-21).

Joshua	As the successor to Moses, Joshua led the nation of Israel into the Promised Land. He is most famous for winning the battle of Jericho (Deuteronomy 34:9).
Mary	The mother of Jesus, Mary was chosen by God to bring Jesus into the world. She was a virgin when the Holy Spirit came upon her. She humbly submitted to the will of God (Luke 1:38).
Moses	As the author of the first five books of the Bible, Moses is the dominant character in the Old Testament. He is the first leader of the Israelite nation. Under his leadership, God led the people out of slavery to the threshold of the Promised Land. *And there has not arisen a prophet since in Israel like Moses* (Deuteronomy 34:10).
Noah	Chosen to build an ark (large boat), Noah was a righteous man in a period when evil was rampant. The ark protected many animals along with his family from the devastation of a world-wide flood (Genesis 6:9).
Paul	The New Testament introduces Paul as Saul of Tarsus, a violent man who persecuted followers of Jesus. His name changed after his encounter with Jesus. He was called to be an apostle to the Gentiles. Paul's missionary journeys are detailed in the book of Acts and he wrote over a dozen New Testament books (I Timothy 1:12-14).
Peter	The brother of Andrew, Peter is perhaps the most famous apostle of Jesus. He is remembered for denying that he knew Jesus and preaching the first sermon on the day the church began (Acts 2:14-36).
Pharisees	A group of Jews who prided themselves on keeping religious rules and rituals while ignoring the important matters of faith, justice and mercy. Jesus considered them hypocrites and blind guides. He warned his disciples to do as they say, but not as they do (Matthew 23:3).
Philip	One of the twelve apostles, Philip is famous for informing Jesus that they did not have enough money to feed the multitudes in John 6.

Samson	An early Israelite hero, Samson was a judge used to assist God's people in their struggle against the Philistines. He is known for having great strength, but also for compromising with foreign women (Judges 16).
Samuel	Before he was born, Samuel was given to the Lord by his mother. He was raised in the temple and had a tender heart toward God. He anointed Saul and David, the first two kings of Israel (I Samuel 10:1; 16:1).
Sarah	Abraham's wife and Isaac's mother, Sarah is regarded in Scripture as a model of godly submission (I Peter 3:1-6).
Simeon	A devout Jew, Simeon was told by the Holy Spirit that he would not die until he had seen the Messiah. He held baby Jesus in his arms and praised God that he had seen God's salvation (Luke 2:25-32).
Solomon	The son of King David, Solomon is the third king of Israel. He was known for the wisdom he received from God and wrote most of the book of Proverbs (I Kings 4:25-34).
Zacchaeus	A chief tax collector, Zacchaeus had a personal encounter with Jesus that changed him thoroughly. He promised to give half of his possessions to the poor and pay back four times those he had cheated (Luke 19:1-10).

Endnotes

§

Grateful acknowledgement is made to the following authors and publishers for permission to reprint excerpts from their copyrighted works.

Lesson 1

1. John Stott, *Basic Christianity,* William B. Eerdmans Publishing Company, 1971 second edition, Grand Rapids, Michigan. Used by permission.
2. *Gospel Transformation,* copyright 2001. Extract reprinted with the written permission of World Harvest Mission (www.whm.org). All rights reserved.
3. John Stott, *The World's Challenge to the Church,* Dallas, Texas: *Bibliotheca Sacra,* published by Dallas Seminary, April/June, 1988. Used by permission.

Lesson 2

1. *Imaginary Creatures from another Planet,* as told by Major Ian Thomas, Estes Park, Colorado. Used by permission.

Lesson 3

1. Excerpted from *The Lotus and the Cross,* 2001 by Ravi Zacharias. Used by permission of Multnomah Publishers Inc.
2. *The Divine Visitor,* 2005 by Jack Hayford. (Excerpts from pp.1-3) Used by permission of Integrity Publishers, Franklin, Tennessee.

Lesson 4

1. Lee Strobel, *The Case for Easter,* Zondervan, Grand Rapids, Michigan, 2003. Used by permission.

2. John Stott, *The Cross of Christ,* InterVarsity Press, Downers Grove, Illinois, 1986. Used by permission.
3. Reprinted from *The Holy Spirit Power from on High,* by A. B. Simpson, 1895, 1994 Revised Edition, by Zur Ltd. Used by permission of WingSpread Publishers, a division of Zur Ltd., 800.884.4571.

Lesson 5

1. Excerpted from *The Signature of Jesus,* 1988, 1992, 1996 by Brennan Manning. Used by permission of Multnomah Publishers Inc.
2. Taken from *Classic Christianity,* by Bob George, 2000 by Harvest House Publishers, Eugene, Oregon. Used by permission.
3. Kelly Willard, *Cares Chorus,* copyright 1978 Maranatha Praise, Inc. / ASCAP (Administered by Music Services) All Rights Reserved. Used by permission.
4. Tim Hansel, *What Kids Need Most in a Dad,* 1984 Baker Publishing Group, Grand Rapids, Michigan.

Lesson 6

1. Excerpted from *The Ragamuffin Gospel,* 1990, 2000, 2005 by Brennan Manning. Used by permission of Multnomah Publishers Inc.
2. R. T. Kendall, *Total Forgiveness,* 2002, Charisma House, a part of Strang Communications Company, Lake Mary, Florida. (Excerpts from pp. 11-60) Used by permission.
3. Max Lucado, *In the Grip of Grace,* 1996, Published in Nashville, Tennessee by Thomas Nelson, Inc.

Lesson 7

1. Reprinted from *Whatever Happened to Worship?,* by A.W. Tozer, 1985 by Zur Ltd. Used by permission of WingSpread Publishers, a division of Zur Ltd., 800.884.4571.
2. Reprinted from *The Pursuit of Man,* by A. W. Tozer, 1950, 1978, by Zur Ltd. Used by permission of WingSpread Publishers, a division of Zur Ltd., 800.884.4571.
3. Extract from *Christian Basics,* copyright 1991, 1999, 2003, by John R.W. Stott. Reproduced with permission of Lion Hudson, plc.
4. Reprinted from *The Pursuit of Man,* by A. W. Tozer, 1950, 1978, by Zur Ltd. Used by permission of WingSpread Publishers, a division of Zur Ltd., 800.884.4571.
5. Reprinted from *The Christ of the Forty Days,* by A. B. Simpson, 1890, 1995 Revised Eby Zur Ltd. Used by permission of WingSpread Publishers, a division of Zur Ltd., 800.884.4571.

6. E. M. Bounds, *Power Through Prayer,* 1982, Baker Publishing Group, Grand Rapids, Michigan.
7. Reprinted from *Wholly Sanctified,* by A. B. Simpson, 1891, 1991 Revised Edition by Zur Ltd. Used by permission of WingSpread Publishers, a division of Zur Ltd., 800.884.4571.

Lesson 8

1. Ron Bennett, *Intentional Disciplemaking,* NavPress, 2001, Colorado Springs, Colorado. Used by permission.
2. Reprinted from *Christ in You,* by A. B. Simpson, 1997 by Zur Ltd. Used by permission of WingSpread Publishers, a division of Zur Ltd., 800.884.4571. (previously published as *The Christ Life,* 1888, and *The Self Life and the Christ Life,* 1897)
3. Reprinted from *That Incredible Christian,* by A. W. Tozer; 1964, by Zur Ltd. Used by permission WingSpread Publishers, a division of Zur Ltd., 800.884.4571
4. Reprinted from *The Pursuit of God,* by A. W. Tozer, 1948, 1982, 1993 by Zur Ltd. Used by permission of WingSpread Publishers, a division of Zur Ltd., 800.884.4571.

Lesson 9

1. Taken from *The Life You've Always Wanted,* by John Ortberg. Copyright 1997 by John Ortberg. Used by permission of Zondervan.
2. Reprinted from *Paths to Power,* by A. W. Tozer, 1940 by Zur Ltd. Used by permission of WingSpread Publishers, a division of Zur Ltd., 800.884.4571.
3. Ray Ortlund, *When God Comes to Church,* Baker Publishing Group, Grand Rapids, Michigan.
4. Reprinted from *Wingspread,* by A. W. Tozer, 1943 by Zur Ltd. Used by permission of WingSpread Publishers, a division of Zur Ltd., 800.884.4571.

Lesson 10

1. *Before We Kill and Eat You,* by Henry Garlock, pp. 73, 74, 76. Copyright 2003, Regal Books, Ventura California. Used by permission.
2. John Stott, *Christ the Controversialist,* InterVarsity Press, Downers Grove, Illinois, 1970. Quoted in John Stott, *Authentic Christianity,* InterVarsity Press, Downers Grove, Illinois, 1996.
3. *Millionaire in New York* reprinted from *Wholly Sanctified,* by A. B. Simpson, 1891, 1991 Revised edition by Zur Ltd. Used by permission of WingSpread Publishers, a division of Zur Ltd., 800.884.4571.

Lesson 11

1. J. Allan Petersen, *The Myth of the Greener Grass,* Tyndale House Publishers Inc., Wheaton, Illinois, 1983. Used by permission.
2. John Stott, *Basic Christianity,* William B. Eerdmans Publishing Company, 1971 second edition, Grand Rapids, Michigan. Used by permission.
3. *Addicted to Love,* by Stephen Arterburn, Servant Publications, 1991. Used by permission.
4. Robert Wolgemuth. Taken from *The Most Important Year in a Woman's Life / The Most Important Year in a Man's Life* by Robert D. Wolgemuth; Mark DeVries; Barbara J. Wolgemuth; Susan Devries. Copyright 2003 by Barbara J. Wolgemuth and Susand DeVries 2003 by Robert D. Wolgemuth and Mark DeVries. Used by permission of Zondervan.

Lesson 12

1. Erwin Raphael McManus, *An Unstoppable Force,* pp. 23, Group Publishing Inc., Loveland, Colorado, 2001. Used by permission.
2. E. M. Bounds, *Power Through Prayer,* 1982, Baker Publishing Group, Grand Rapids, Michigan.
3. Gordon MacDonald, *Restoring Your Spiritual Passion,* Oliver Nelson Books, a division of Thomas Nelson, Inc., Nashville, Tennessee, 1986. Used by permission.

Lesson 13

1. Eugene Peterson, *Eat This Book,* William B. Eerdmans Publishing Company, Grand Rapids, Michigan, 2006. Published in association with the literary agency of Alive Communications Inc., Colorado Springs, Colorado.
2. Reprinted from *We Travel an Appointed Way,* by A. W. Tozer, 1988 by Zur Ltd. Used by permission of WingSpread Publishers, a division of Zur Ltd., 800.884.4571.
3. Taken from *Fresh Power* by Jim Cymbala; Dean Merrill. Copyright 2001 by Jim Cymbala. Used by permission of Zondervan.
4. Morton Thompson, *The Cry and the Covenant,* Copyright 1949. Published in arrangement with Doubleday and Company Inc., a division of Random House, Inc.
5. *Suen Douh Camp Purchased for $1.00,* as told by John Bechtel, West Palm Beach, Florida. Used by permission.

CPSIA information can be obtained
at www.ICGtesting.com
Printed in the USA
BVHW051345151120
593068BV00013B/349